GEMS OF INDIA

SKETCHES OF DISTINGUISHED HINDOO AND MAHOMEDAN WOMEN

E. J. HUMPHREY

GYAN

Published by

Gyan Publishing House
5, Ansari Road
Daryaganj, New Delhi-110002
Phone: 011-47034999, 9811692060
E-mail: books@gyanbooks.com

Distribution Network
gyanbooks.com
India, USA, Canada, UK, Australia

ISBN: 978-93-7097-199-8 (PB)

First Published, 1875

2nd Impression 2025

Printed at: Gyan Press, Delhi.

GEMS OF INDIA
Author E. J. Humphrey

GEMS OF INDIA

The Taj Mahal.

GEMS OF INDIA;

OR,

Sketches of Distinguished Hindoo and Mahomedan Women.

BY MRS. E. J. HUMPHREY.

FOUR ILLUSTRATIONS.

NEW YORK:
NELSON & PHILLIPS.
CINCINNATI: HITCHCOCK & WALDEN.
1875.

TO

AMERICAN WOMEN,

OF WHATEVER RELIGIOUS DENOMINATION OR CREED,

I Dedicate this Work,

WITH THE PRAYER AND HOPE THAT FROM PERUSING IT THE INTEREST THEY ALREADY TAKE IN THE WOMEN OF HEATHEN LANDS MAY BE GREATLY INCREASED.

Preface.

EVER since the Taj Mahal, that incomparable mausoleum of Mumtaz Mahal, the lovely and beloved queen of Shah Jahan, met my vision, a new interest in the women of India was kindled in my mind, and I resolved to make their past and present condition and capabilities matters of study and research as far as practicable; but, amid the manifold cares, labors, and illnesses incident to missionary life in the trying climate of India, I found but little opportunity to carry out my resolve.

From time to time, however, when items of interest came in my way, I made memoranda, which, with the information given in authentic histories, and the traditions of the people, have enabled me to gather material for these sketches.

It is always difficult to find reliable accounts of the characters of even distinguished persons after the lapse of busy centuries, and this is particularly the case in India on account of the national proclivity to indulge in the mythical and the marvelous.

Several of the sketches are, therefore, unavoidably meager in details of personal characteristics, and the capabilities of the subjects are brought out mostly by historical incidents, which show their conduct under certain circumstances.

I hope, however, that the glimpses of the history of the country, from the beginning of the Mahomedan period to the present time, which these sketches afford, will not only be interesting to the reader, but will awaken a desire to become better acquainted with the strange and thrilling history of that rich and brilliant, but most unhappy and unfortunate, land, which has so long been suffered to remain enshrouded in the thick darkness of heathen superstition, but is now, in God's own good time, visited by the light of the glorious Gospel of Christ.

I have endeavored to always make the line between authentic history and tradition so plain that it may be apparent at the first glance, so that no unnecessary draught be made upon the reader's credulity.

I was particularly assisted in the sketches of Hindoo women by an article that appeared in the "Calcutta Review" a few years ago, and in the sketch of the Begums of Bhopal by a book published under the direction of the Sikandar Begum herself, giving a minute account of her pilgrimage to Mecca.

I have also consulted guide books, and four of the best histories of India extant, but have depended mainly for dates upon Marshman.

E. J. H.

CONTENTS.

PAGE
SANJOGATA, THE LAST RANEE OF DELHI 11
PUDMUNEE, THE BEAUTIFUL CINGALESE 21
DURGAVATEE, THE WARRIOR RANEE—A CHAPTER OF MOGUL HISTORY 32
JODH BAIE, THE HINDOO SULTANA—A CHAPTER OF MOGUL HISTORY 40
CHAND SULTANA—A CHAPTER OF MOGUL HISTORY 52
NOOR MAHAL, THE LIGHT OF THE PALACE—A CHAPTER OF MOGUL HISTORY 65
MUMTAZ MAHAL—A CHAPTER OF MOGUL HISTORY 91
AHULIYA BAIE, THE MAHRATTEE QUEEN 111
KISHNA COMAREE BAIE; OR, THE MAIDEN'S SACRIFICE 127
THE RANEE OF JHANSEE—A TALE OF THE INDIAN MUTINY 140
THE BEGUMS OF BHOPAL 153
THE WOMEN OF INDIA 176

Illustrations.

THE TAJ MAHAL 2
NOOR MAHAL 64
MUMTAZ MAHAL 90
THE BEGUM OF BHOPAL 152

GEMS OF INDIA.

SANJOGATA,

The Last Ranee of Delhi.

OUR first sketch is of long ago, when the American continent was only known to its own wild inhabitants, and England was just beginning to emerge from barbarism.

King Richard I., the famous crusader, reigned over England from A. D. 1189 to 1199. Upon his death the treacherous John ascended the throne, from whom the famous *Magna Charta* was wrung by an exasperated and persistent people. About this time, that is, the close of the twelfth and the beginning of the thirteenth century, Hindoostan was literally what its name signifies—the place or country of the Hindoos. The whole extent of country north of the Vindhya range of mountains was divided into petty kingdoms, governed by Rajas possessing more or less power, according to the customs and laws of the different castes. The four largest and most prosperous kingdoms were those of Delhi, or Yoginipoor, as it was then called, which was held by the division of Hindoos called Tomara, Ajmere by that of Chauhan, Canauj by the one called Rathore, and Guzerat by the Bagheelas.

The Raja of Delhi had no male children, and, about A. D. 1180, adopted his grandson, Prithwi, the young Raja of Ajmere, so that Delhi and Ajmere, the Tomaras and Chauhans, were united under one government.

The Raja of Canauj was also a grandson of the Raja of Delhi, and had been indulging secretly the hope of one day inheriting his throne. He was, of course, greatly disappointed and enraged when the preference was given to his cousin, the Raja of Ajmere, and after the death of the grandfather rivalries and wars became the order of the day between the two kingdoms. This unhappy state of things greatly accelerated the progress of the Mahomedans, who were slowly but surely encroaching upon the north-western frontier of Hindoostan.

The kingdom of Canauj included Nepal, in the Himalayas, and extended as far west as the rivers Chumbul and Bunas, and—the Hindoos claim—even to the Indus. Its capital, the city of Canauj, was situated on the Ganges river, about midway between Cawnpore and Futtaghur. Both Hindoo and Mahomedan writers extol the beauty and magnificence of this city, whose glories have long since passed away. It is described as "a city which raised its head to the skies, and in strength and beauty might boast of being unrivaled."

Sanjogata, the subject of this sketch, was the daughter of Jaichand, the Raja of Canauj. Hindoo writers represent her to have been of great personal beauty, and of superior intelligence and amiability. When the troublesome feud broke out between her father and the Raja of Delhi, Sanjogata was just blooming into womanhood and was yet unmarried. This fact shows us that the objectionably early marriages now customary among the Hindoos were not general at that period.

The Moslem invaders had not yet frightened the people by their lawlessness into the practice of keeping their women in seclusion, and a fair degree of liberty was allowed them. It seems probable, too, that they even had some power of choice in regard to their husbands granted them.

Soon after the accession of Prithwi, or Prithiraj, as he was then called, he gave a series of brilliant entertainments in honor of the event. By the coalition of the two governments he had become ruler of a much larger kingdom than would otherwise have been under his sway. His name, Prithwi, signifying *earth*, was, therefore, joined to the title of Raja, slightly abbreviated, so that his name and title joined formed the high-sounding cognomen of "King of the Earth." It was also a clever way of avoiding a dispute as to whether he should be called the Raja of Delhi or Ajmere. The rejoicings progressed merrily, and were concluded by a peculiar and expensive religious festival, called the Aswamedha. The Raja of Canauj was filled with bitterness, envy, and rancor, and resolved by one grand outlay to outshine his young rival. To this intent he made preparations to celebrate a most ancient and sacred Hindoo festival, called the Rajshui, which, in order to be perfect, must be participated in by all Hindoo princes living at the time.

Prithiraj, of course, was not invited to the celebration, and another young Raja, a friend of his, was also slighted. Their places were filled by their effigies, made of gold, and Raja Jaichand strove to heap obloquy upon them by assigning to the effigy of Prithiraj the post of porter, and to his friend that of scullion, in the hall of sacrifice. He also planned to give interest to the occasion by allowing his beautiful daughter to choose her husband from among the assembled princes. At the close of the religious ceremonies she was to be led through the hall to choose her future lord, and was to signify her choice by throwing a necklace of flowers, called the barmala, or marriage garland, around the neck of the fortunate prince. The marriage ceremonies, conducted with all the pomp and splendor possible, were to conclude the great festival, after which the Raja could rest satisfied that he had outdone his rival, even though that rival was ruler of two kingdoms.

But, alas for the certainty of even royal plans! The princess Sanjogata, like her mother, Eve, had thought a great deal on forbidden subjects, and having heard rumors of the beauty and gallant conduct of Prithiraj, had in her heart resolved that he should be her choice.

She kept her own counsel, however, until the right time for action arrived, then, without allowing herself to think of the sorrow she would cause her aged father by her willfulness, she walked quietly along when led through the long lines of anxious and expectant princes, until, having reached the door where stood the golden effigy of Prithiraj, she threw the garland around its neck!

The confusion and dismay of the assemblage were overwhelming. The poor old Raja was overcome by chagrin at having his plans for triumphing over his rival so unceremoniously overturned by his own daughter; but there was no help for it, and the festival was hastily and sadly concluded. Our princess must have been in dire disgrace, but probably her romantic attachment to the prince she had never seen kept her from yielding to despondency. She seems to have been one of those sporadic champions of woman's rights who are scattered here and there through the annals of the past; but we would scarcely expect that such independent action in a Hindoo princess of the thirteenth century would be unchecked and unpunished.

Of course the Raja of Delhi was informed in due time of his rival's discomfiture, and the preference so openly expressed for himself by his courageous daughter, and, like a true knight of "ye olden tyme," he quickly made a bold raid upon the court of the Raja of Canauj, and succeeded in carrying the princess off in open day. They were hotly pursued, but reached Delhi in safety, where their marriage was celebrated amid great rejoicing. For one short year they enjoyed uninterrupted happiness, but at its close their luxurious life was suddenly broken in upon by the re-appearance of the dreaded Mahomedan army upon the frontier. Shabab-oo-Deen had advanced upon Delhi two years previous, and had been repulsed; but now, with large reinforcements, he again marched upon the royal city.

Sanjogata encouraged her husband to defend his capital bravely. She begged him not to think of his own life, or of her, but to do his duty, remembering that "to die well is to live forever." "Let your sword divide your foe," she said, "and I will be your partner in the future life." Probably she meant by this that if he should fall she would not long survive him.

The Raja hastened to call a council of war and to notify his allies, and shortly all was in readiness to begin the campaign.

It was the custom among the Hindoos of old, that when the head of a family went forth to battle he took solemn leave of all his female relatives, who exhorted him as he left to be courageous and brave.

Sanjogata performed her part in this ceremony with fortitude and enthusiasm until—as was customary—she endeavored to fasten the helmet that hid the face of her beloved husband. A presentiment seized her that she would never gaze upon his countenance again, and she became so agitated with grief that she could not secure the clasps. Another had to perform this office, and the Raja, with one last glance and a cheerful farewell, hastened to his place at the head of his army. Sanjogata gazed sadly after him and exclaimed: "I shall never see him again in Yoginipoor, (Delhi,) but in the region of Swarga (heaven) I shall again behold him!"

Her presentiment was correct. The Hindoo army was routed, and Prithiraj, the last Raja of Delhi, was slain upon the field. Sanjogata fasted and wept during the progress of the conflict, and when convinced that the Raja had indeed fallen, she ordered a pyre to be erected and was burned upon it, deeming this the surest and readiest means of rejoining her husband.

This is the first authentic instance of "Suttee," or widow-burning, mentioned in Hindoo writings, but probably the custom prevailed to some extent before this time. It would seem, however, that it was only to be followed *voluntarily*.

Poor unfortunate princess! Ignorant of the God of love and all comfort, her yearning love for her slaughtered husband led her to forestall the day when by a natural death she might rejoin him, by giving herself in the bloom of life to the flames. We can admire the devotion of this brave young creature, while we lament the ignorance and superstition that led to this fearful act of self-sacrifice.

She was the last Ranee who reigned in Yoginipoor, and with the close of her short career was Hindoo power in Delhi ended.

Shabab-oo-Deen did not remain long in Hindoostan, but he left a favorite slave, named Kutub-oo-Deen, upon the throne of Delhi, who founded the dynasty of the Slave kings. This Mahomedan ruler began the building of the famous pillar named after him, the Kutub Minar. It stands about eleven miles from the present city of Delhi, the intervening space being covered with mounds and ruins of the old city, the Yoginipoor of the Hindoos. According to Hindoo tradition the Kutub Minar was begun by Prithiraj for the use of his young bride, that she might every morning view from its summit the river Jumna, several miles distant.

Sanjogata, it seems, was a worshiper of the sun, and the river Jumna is supposed to be a daughter of that luminary, and the fair idolatress could thus pay her devotions to both divinities at the same time. Mahomedans, of course, deny this, and say it was designed and built in commemoration of the establishment of Moslem power in Hindoostan. It was completed by Altamash-oo-Deen, the son-in-law and successor of Kutub-oo-Deen, about 1235. It is said to have been much higher than at present, but after the lapse of six centuries it is difficult to ascertain facts of detail. It is now two hundred and thirty-eight feet above the level of the ground, and is wholly unconnected with any other building. The diameter of the base is forty-seven feet two inches, with an upper diameter of nearly nine feet. There are five stories and five galleries, including the one at the top. The building is nearly all of red sandstone, and has a spiral staircase within of the same material extending to the top. The lowest story is covered with flutings alternately angular and circular; on the second story the flutings are all circular, and on the third angular.

The fourth section is faced with marble, having a belt of dark stone at the bottom; and the fifth is of sandstone, with two belts of marble, and some ornamental work in marble close to the summit. On the top is an iron railing. It has suffered from earthquakes somewhat, and on this account a cupola that crowned its summit was taken down early in the present century, when the British Government had the whole structure put in perfect repair, at an outlay of over twenty thousand pounds. The cupola stands near the great pillar, in a much humbler but safer position than formerly. A lightning conductor is now attached to the pillar, which, it is hoped, will prevent any farther injury from this source.

It is wonderful that such a high and isolated structure—the highest single pillar in the world—has withstood the sirocco blasts and the rainy seasons of over six hundred years!

The conquest of Delhi and Ajmere by the Mahomedans was followed the succeeding year (1193) by that of Canauj, and shortly after by that of the remaining Hindoo principalities, and the rule of the Crescent remained in force in Hindoostan until 1757, when it too, in its turn, was overcome and destroyed by the English power, and a brighter day dawned upon the long oppressed and benighted races of Hindoostan.

Yoginipoor is partly covered with the ruins of yet another ruined city, and the site of the once surpassingly beautiful city of Canauj can scarcely be identified.

"*Sic transit gloria mundi.*"

PUDMUNEE,

The Beautiful Cingalese.

OUR next heroine was originally a citizen of the Cinnamon Isle, that lovely palm-fringed Eden, which no one who has seen can ever forget.

Pudmunee, the daughter of Hameer Lunk, one of the kings of Ceylon, or Lunka, lived at the close of the thirteenth century, and met a tragical death A. D. 1303.

Only women of beauty and amiability bear the name of Pudmunee, which is the highest of the four class-names bestowed upon Hindoo females. The name is from Pudma, the goddess of riches.

The second class-name is Chitrinee, from *chit*, the heart, and was probably given to women who were distinguished by those qualities that win hearts, more than for personal beauty.

The other two names, Sankhinee and Hastinee, are given to women of harsh and unlovely dispositions and plain features. The last name is, in fact, that of a female elephant, and must have been considered a term of great reproach.

Of course, in those days Ceylon was not under the British rule. Colombo, Galle, and other cities, at least in their present state, with their fine public buildings, and immense shipping in their harbors; the coffee and cinnamon plantations and the railway, did not then exist.

All these adjuncts of civilization were brought in by the white-faced foreigners. But Lunka, the land of abundance, must have been surpassingly beautiful even in its primitive state. With its many kinds of palm-trees; its valleys and mountains, covered with wild cinnamon, coffee, and rice; its numerous fruits, extreme fertility, and small demand for labor, it is no wonder that when the Mahomedans discovered it they deemed it the veritable site of the garden of Eden, where "out of the ground made the Lord God to grow every tree that is pleasant to the sight, and good for food."

Ceylon is also rich in gems and pearls, or rather was so in those days; but the latter have grown scarce of late, and the British Government has been obliged to protect the pearl fisheries by prohibiting their use and keeping strict guard over them, in the hope that they may in time regain their former value.

It is supposed that Ceylon is part of the country known to the Hebrews as Ophir. It is called pearliform, and is really shaped like the old style ear-drop, and looks on the map like a pendant of Hindoostan. It is a small island two hundred and seventy miles long by two hundred and forty in width, with a circumference of seven hundred and sixty miles; latitude 5° 53′ to 9° 51″ North, longitude 79 41′ 40″ to 81′ 54′ 50″ East. The sun rises about five and a half hours earlier than in England. Light from six to six nearly all the year round; about half an hour longer in June than in December. The interior of the island is very mountainous, affording fine sanitaria for the European residents. Kandy, formerly the capital of a fierce and warlike tribe of heathens, is a place of frequent resort. It is only one thousand six hundred and seventy feet above the level of the sea, and the heat during the day is as great as at Colombo, but the nights are cool and refreshing. It has a lovely artificial lake, which adds greatly to the attractiveness of the place.

Newera Ellia, another sanitarium, is much higher, the mountains in its neighborhood varying from seven thousand to eight thousand feet in height.

Adam's Peak, or Samanala, a mountain seven thousand three hundred and fifty-two feet above the sea level, is the most celebrated part of the island. The Mahomedans gave the first-mentioned name to the mountain. They believe that Adam stood on the top of it to take a farewell look of his beloved Eden, fairer than ever as he saw it for the last time, and then, when God spake the word that expelled him from Paradise, he sprang off the mountain and crossed over by a ledge of rocks, called "Adam's Bridge," to the continent, leaving the impress of his last footstep on the top of the mountain. There certainly is a cavity on the peak, said to be a little less than a cubit in length, and by the exercise of a great deal of faith and imagination it might be called a footprint. A Mahomedan writer calls the two roads leading to the top of this mountain the paths of papa and mamma Adam and Eve.

The Hindoos also regard the mountain as sacred. They call it Swargahanam, that is, the ascent to heaven. The mysterious footprint was made, they say, by the burning foot of Shiva, the destroyer.

But to the Buddhists this mountain is pre-eminently sacred and precious. According to their traditions Buddha, their god, *flew* from Ceylon across the Bay of Bengal to Siam. Rising from a spot near Colombo, he passed over this mountain, resting one foot for a moment on its top, leaving its impress as a seal to show that Lanka is the inheritance of Buddha.

The Buddhists gave the name Samanala to the mountain from a supposed demon call Saman, who lived at its base. Mahomedans, Hindoos, and Budhists, from Ceylon and the southern portion of the continent, make annual pilgrimages to Adam's Peak, but only the Buddhists have a temple upon the mountain.

How vain appear all these traditions to the Christian, and yet they show us how strong is the tendency of the human heart to search out and worship some mysterious principle or being who is all-pervading and all-powerful!

How strange it seems that the light which we are told "lighteth every man that cometh into the world," does not show to the teeming millions of India and beautiful Ceylon the holy and divine nature of the great God who created so much beauty and grandeur!

We sing that sublime missionary hymn of the sainted Heber; but one must see the lovely island of Ceylon and its thousands of heathen inhabitants, who never "look through nature up to nature's God," but content themselves with the senseless follies of idolatry, in order to fully appreciate the force of the lines,—

> "What though the spicy breezes
> Blow soft o'er Ceylon's isle;
> Though every prospect pleases,
> And only man is vile:
> In vain with lavish kindness
> The gifts of God are strown;
> The heathen in his blindness
> Bows down to wood and stone,—"

and often the query rises, "How came this state of things to exist?" Is it because the people of old deliberately *chose* darkness rather than light, because they did not like to retain God in their knowledge, and that at last even he wearied of their folly and left them to believe a lie?

We cannot solve the mystery, but we believe there is yet hope for the heathen world, and that many from among these benighted ones shall hear the Gospel message and receive it gladly; when the self-righteous Buddhists and exalted twice-born Brahmin shall, side by side with the despised Sudra and the whilom follower of the false prophet, wash in the fountain that is opened in the house of David for sin and uncleanness, and be born again of water and of the Spirit.

"For as the earth bringeth forth her bud, and as the garden causeth the things that are sown in it to spring forth; so the Lord God will cause righteousness and praise to spring forth before all the nations." . . .

In the thirteenth century intermarriages between Hindoos of the Continent and Ceylon were more frequent than now, and it so came to pass that Pudmunee, the beautiful daughter of Hameer Lunk, who then reigned over a portion of Ceylon, was betrothed, and afterward married, to a prince of Chitore, the uncle and protector of the heir apparent, who was a child.

For a few years Pudmunee lived in peace and happiness with her husband, and grew so beautiful that the fame of her charms spread through all the country round about.

But a dark cloud was even then spreading over the political horizon of Hindoostan, which was destined to bring swift and sure destruction to many a flourishing city and happy home, and among them to the celebrated city of Chitore and the home of Pudmunee.

In the year 1294, a century after the Mahomedans had gained a firm footing in Upper India, Allah-oo-Deen, the nephew, and general of Firoz Shah, the reigning king of Delhi, pursued the Mahomedan conquests across the Nerbudda river into that section of India known as the Deccan, that is, *Dakhan*, the South.

The victorious army of the Moslems halted before Chitore and laid siege to the city. But the Hindoos were well prepared for the siege. In those troublous times the cities were always strongly fortified and well provisioned, and Chitore was no exception to the general rule. The siege was carried on for some time without any impression being made on the city. Finally, according to native traditions, the following singular occurrences took place.

The Mahomedan general sent a flag of truce to the Raja, and, frankly owning that one object of the invasion was to obtain his beautiful Ranee, made this strange proposal. He offered to raise the siege and depart from the country if he might only be permitted to behold the extraordinary beauty of Pudmunee by means of mirrors.

Of course, this request was at first refused, but at length the temptation to get rid of the troublesome invader by this easy way proved too great. The Raja notified the Mahomedan general that his request would be acceded to, and a day was appointed for him to be admitted to the city. He came, attended by only a slight guard, and had his wish gratified. The Raja was pleased by the trust reposed in his honor, shown by the fearlessness of the general in coming into the city with so few attendants; and, to show that he had equal confidence in the integrity of his rival, he accompanied him just outside the gate of the city, Allah-oo-Deen meanwhile occupying his attention by profuse apologies and acknowledgments.

Suddenly, however, the scene changed. A band of soldiers, that had been secreted outside, seized the Raja and hurried him off to the Mahomedan camp. A message was immediately sent to the city, to the effect that the Raja would be given up at once if the people would deliver Pudmunee into the hands of the Mahomedans.

The Hindoos held a council, and with Pudmunee's aid concocted a plan to overreach the wily marauders with their own weapons. They returned answer, that as soon as the Mahomedan army would withdraw from their trenches the Ranee Pudmunee would, with her retinue of maidens and personal property, proceed to their camp. Allah-oo-Deen withdrew from his siege-works immediately, and encamped some distance from the city.

At the time appointed the Ranee, with her *maidens*, as was supposed, and personal effects, left the city in seven hundred palanquins, in each of which was a well-armed soldier. The palanquin bearers, too, although apparently ordinary bearers, were, in reality, all soldiers.

When they reached the camp the palanquins were all deposited within the cloth walls surrounding the tents appointed for the reception of the Ranee. The Hindoo prince was then allowed to take leave of his wife, and half an hour was granted them for a parting interview; but instead of improving the time in this way, they made good their retreat to the city, under the protection of the disguised warriors. Too late Allah-oo-Deen learned that his high-minded foes *could* stoop to stratagem when dealing with rogues.

He then withdrew his army from Chitore, and, after a series of conquests of smaller Hindoo kingdoms, returned to Delhi laden with wealth, the spoils of the cities he had pillaged.

He had been absent from Delhi one year, and on his arrival was met outside the city by his uncle, Firoz Shah. The old king was delighted to meet his nephew, and was patting him affectionately on the cheek, when assassins, whom Allah-oo-Deen had posted in ambush near by, rushed upon him and put him to death.

Allah-oo-Deen hastened on to Delhi and seized upon the throne. He endeavored, by public games and amusements, to make the people forget the crime by means of which he had become their ruler, but he did not succeed. Province after province rebelled, but were all subjugated by his prompt energy. In 1297 he invaded Guzerat, which was, up to this time, governed by Hindoos. He soon swept away every vestige of their power, destroyed the idols in the principal temples, and erected Mahomedan mosques in the most prominent places. The Ranee of Guzerat, a beautiful woman, was taken from her husband and made the queen of the ruthless emperor.

It is evident that Allah-oo-Deen still kept his eye upon Chitore, but owing to the time occupied in conquering Guzerat, and a fierce invasion of the Moguls, who came rushing down upon Delhi like a torrent in 1298, he did not find an opportunity to march upon it until 1303. This time he had an immense army, against which the brave Hindoos of Chitore had no chance of success. They, therefore, resolved that they would all perish.

The women, headed by Pudmunee, still in the bloom of youth, were all burned to death. Historians differ a little in regard to the way in which this was accomplished, but all are agreed as to the fact. English writers say that an immense funeral pyre was erected, and when it was fired all the women threw themselves into the flames. Hindoo historians say that the fire was kindled in a large cavern in the fort, and that all the women of the city, several thousand in number, with the Ranee at their head, then solemnly marched into the cavern, and the door was closed upon them and sealed by their male relations.

Of course, they died almost instantly from suffocation and the flames.

When this dreadful part of the tragedy was complete, the Raja, with his army and the citizens, threw open the gates of the city, fell upon the enemy, and fought desperately until all obtained the death they sought.

The Mahomedans, enraged by thus losing all their human prey, destroyed the whole city, except the royal residence, where the Raja and his beautiful Ranee had resided. It was spared out of respect to her memory.

Thus ended the brief life of Pudmunee the beautiful. Her sad story is related by Hindoo parents to their children up to the present time, and as they grieve over Hindoo supremacy, so long passed away, they weep for the beautiful woman who, with thousands of others, passed away with it in a chariot of fire.

DURGAVATEE,

The Warrior Ranee—A Chapter of Mogul History.

TWO hundred and more years had passed away since the occurrences of our last sketch took place. Meanwhile Hindoostan had been a great theater of wars and intrigues.

The Mahomedan power was superseded, in 1526, by the Mogul emperor Baber, the sixth in descent from Tamerlane the Great. The Moguls were originally worshipers of the *Delay Lama*, but when they emerged from their mountain fastnesses in Mongolia, and began their career of depredation, they seemed to leave all pretense of religion behind them. Afterward, however, when they mingled with Mahomedans they professed that faith, and, although always more liberal in their views than the orthodox faithful, they were counted as true believers.

Time passed on. Baber died in 1530, and was succeeded on the throne of Delhi by his son Humayoon, who, after a tempestuous and broken reign, accidentally met his death in 1556. His son, the renowned Akbar, was crowned emperor when but a lad, and for fifty-one years reigned over the greater portion of Hindoostan.

It was in 1564 that Asof Jah, one of Akbar's

generals, was sent down into the Deccan to conquer the little province of Gurrah, that had hitherto maintained its independence. It was then governed by a Ranee who must have been a widow, as no mention is made of her husband in connection with this invasion and the disasters that followed. She was acting as regent, as the heir was a child. She was a daughter of the Raja of Mahoba, the capital of the province of Bandulkund, and was very beautiful and accomplished. What those accomplishments were we can only guess. Probably she could read and write, and was well versed in the poetical histories of the gods.

When she became of marriageable age her hand was sought by the Goand king of Gurrah, which territory is now included in the provinces of Sangor and Nerbudda. But the tribe of Chandails, to whom Durgavatee belonged, was a very proud caste of Rajputs, and her father, the Raja of Mahoba, was not favorable to the suitor because he was one of the aboriginal kings, and could not claim affinity with the sacred twice-born Brahmins. He did not like, however, to reject him outright, and so provoke his enmity, and, perhaps, bring an invading army into his own dominions; so he cast about in his mind for conditions that he might impose, which would be very difficult for the Goand king to fulfill.

After mature deliberation, befitting the dignity of such a high-born and lofty being, the Raja of Mahoba returned answer to the king of Gurrah that when he should come with an army of fifty thousand men he would receive the hand of the Princess Durgavatee in marriage. He thought it would be quite impossible for the poor aboriginal king to gather such an army. Surely the gods would never allow an outcast to have resources equal to that!

The Mahoba Raja thought he had surely done an uncommonly clever thing to find so easy a road out of his difficulties. But, alas for human arrogance! the ruler of Gurrah had larger resources than his neighbors dreamed of, and after a little drafting and bribery he succeeded in gathering an army of fifty thousand strong. Of course, he lost no time in marching to the capital of Bandulkund and claiming his promised bride, and as the condition imposed had been fully met, the Princess Durgavatee shortly afterward departed with her husband to his dominions. How long the Raja of Gurrah lived after the marriage does not appear, but probably only a few years, and Durgavatee was left to rule over the province until her son should attain his majority.

It is stated that at this period the province was three hundred miles in length and one hundred in breadth, and that there were about seventy thousand populous towns and villages which had never fallen under the dominion of foreigners, not even of the Hindoos. There are but few vestiges of such prosperity now remaining, but it is certain that the province was at least rich enough to tempt the cupidity of the victorious Moguls.

Great was the alarm in the peaceful, happy country when it was rumored that Akbar's army was marching to invade it. The people must have known well that there was but little hope of success in attempting to cope with the powerful Mogul legions, and there is something pitiful in the sight of a little province like this being swallowed up by an overwhelming force while bravely defending themselves to the last. This they had determined to do, and an army of fifteen hundred elephants, eight thousand horse, and some infantry, was put in order and sent forth to repel the invading Moguls as best they might. The regent, Durgavatee, led her troops on to action. She was mounted in a howdah, on a fine elephant, and was clothed in armor, with a helmet upon her head and a burnished lance in her hand. A bow and quiver lay by her side.

Her appearance at their head roused all the chivalry of the army, and, added to the love of national independence, inspired every heart with courage and enthusiasm. They fought bravely, and twice routed the Mogul army, laying six hundred of their horsemen dead on the field. Then night came on and both parties retired from the field. The Ranee wished to continue the assault, and not allow the Moguls time to recover from their discomfiture; but her generals did not think best to follow her advice. This delay was a

3

fatal error, as it gave time for the Moguls to bring up their artillery, that had been detained on account of the bad roads.

Thus reinforced, and extremely anxious to wipe out the disgrace of being twice driven back by troops commanded by a woman, Asof Jah ordered his army to advance in the early morning. The Ranee, with a chosen band of men, disputed his progress at a narrow pass that opened the way to her capital; but they were forced to retreat from their position, as they were so fully exposed to the fire of the artillery.

The Moguls then rushed through the defile into the plain beyond, where the defending army was drawn up in order of battle, and made a vigorous onslaught. They were repulsed, however, by a desperate party headed by the young Raja, who gallantly urged them on to defend their country. Once and again they beat back the Mogul hordes, and for the third time were successfully meeting their attack, when the brave young Raja was wounded so severely that his mother saw he would soon expire from loss of blood. She ordered him to be carried to the rear, where his wounds could be stanched, and the movement of a few to obey her orders gave a welcome and plausible excuse to those of the army who were becoming dispirited to quit the field. They rushed hither and thither in disorder, as if they supposed a retreat had been ordered, and finally the unfortunate

Ranee was left with only three hundred men to face the whole Mogul army. She disdained to fly, and bravely directed her little band of faithful men until she was wounded in the eye by an arrow. She attempted to draw it out, but part of the steel point broke off and remained. Just then another arrow passed through the neck of the poor queen, but this she extricated intact. But nature could not endure as her courageous spirit dictated. Her eyes grew dim, a deadly faintness came over her, and she began to sway from side to side in the howdah. One of her faithful officers begged permission to take her from the field, but she refused to allow him to do so. "We are overcome in battle," she said, "but we will not yield ourselves up to our enemies; let your gratitude and love now incite you to do that service for me for which I lifted up your head, and which I now require at your hands. Hasten, I say, and let your dagger save me from putting an end to my own existence."

The officer burst into tears, and begged that as the elephant was a very fleet one, he might attempt to carry her to a place of safety. At this juncture the enemy began to close round the elephant, and the Ranee, fearing to be taken alive, seized the officer's dagger and plunged it into her heart. Thus bravely and unflinchingly died the Ranee Durgavatee. Six of her highest officers fought like tigers to avenge her death, and would neither give nor accept quarter. They were at last cut down by overwhelming numbers.

A monument to the Ranee Durgavatee stands in the narrow defile where she defended herself and her country so bravely but unsuccessfully. A pair of large rounded stones, which stand near the monument, are supposed by the people to be her two royal drums turned into stone, and it is rumored that they often resound at midnight, and call the spirits of the departed warriors together. It is the custom of travelers who pass by this spot to gather some of the crystals with which the place abounds, and place the finest specimens upon the monument. Near this memorable place flows the beautiful Nerbudda river, whose marble rocks call forth the wonder and admiration of countless travelers from every nation and clime, and whose bed is paved with lovely agates, many of which are covered by nature's photography (it is supposed) with rare moss and foliage.

The Mogul power was for a long time in the ascendant through these valleys and upon these mountains, but it yielded at last to the no less overbearing rule of the Mahrattas, and they in their turn were overthrown by the all-conquering English.

But, amid all these changes, the virtues and courageous spirit of the Ranee Durgavatee have been kept in memory, and held in veneration by the scattered remnants of the Goand tribe, and have been perpetuated by their historians and poets.

The foregoing story shows conclusively that Hindoo females possess as noble and heroic qualities as those of any age or nation.

A Roman or a Christian queen could not have acted more discreetly and courageously than the Ranee Durgavatee. The rudeness and barbarity of the age rendered it necessary that the defeated party should either die, or live to suffer all the dishonor and ignominy that unfeeling and base men might inflict. Hence it is no wonder that the brave young queen preferred to die even by her own hand than live to endure a dishonored existence.

There were instances where English women chose death rather than life during the Indian Mutiny of 1857, and, when the decisive hour came, demanded death at the hands of their husbands or brothers, that they might not fall into the hands of the Sepoys. They were upheld in their hour of agony by the blessed hopes of the Christian faith, but no such help had Durgavatee in her extremity.

If a *heathen* queen could act her part so well, what may not her countrywomen become, and do, when enlightened and elevated by Christianity?

JODH BAIE,

The Hindoo Sultana—A Chapter of Mogul History.

WHEN Baber, the founder of the Mogul dynasty, died, in 1530, his son, Humayoon, became ruler of Hindoostan. The empire was, however, so much weakened by cessions of territory to three younger sons, that the Mahomedan princes of Delhi undertook to expel Humayoon from the throne and the country. They were assisted in this attempt by the Portuguese and the Afghans, and were so successful that Humayoon was a wanderer in the outskirts of India and in Persia for about twenty-five years, when, with the assistance of a Persian army, he was enabled to regain his kingdom.

About eleven years after being driven from Delhi he married a beautiful young girl called Hameedah, who gave birth the succeeding year to a son. This event occurred at a place called Amercot, a fortified Hindoo city, whose ruler was at the time assisting the dethroned monarch with troops and money.

Humayoon was on the march, when the glad tidings that a son was born to him reached him. It is an Eastern custom, upon the birth of a son, for the father to bestow valuable presents upon his relations, friends, and servants ; but the impoverished and fugitive monarch could not, of course, do this, so when all the officers of the army hastened to his tent to offer congratulations, he could only divide a pod of musk among them. He called for a China plate, and, breaking the musk into pieces upon it, remarked : "I can make you no greater present, my noble friends, upon the birth of my son, but I expect his fame will one day fill the world, as the perfume of this musk fills this apartment."

This son was named Jalal-oo-Deen, the "Glory of Faith," and afterward surnamed Akbar, or the "Great." After his birth the fortunes of his father became darker than before, and the royal infant was several times taken prisoner by his paternal uncles, who by this time were also arrayed in antagonism to Humayoon.

In 1555, however, by the help of his Persian allies, the long-exiled king regained his throne, and six months afterward was accidentally killed. He had been sitting on the top of his palace to enjoy the evening air, and was descending the stairs, when the muezzin's call to prayer sounded from the minaret of a neighboring mosque. The king attempted to kneel, to repeat the usual prayer, but his feet became entangled in his long robe, and he fell down the steps, receiving an injury on the head which resulted in death.

This event occurred early in 1556, and Akbar,

then only thirteen years of age, was seated, without serious opposition, upon the throne. For five years he submitted peaceably to the sway of his capable, but ambitious and arrogant, prime minister, Byram Khan, keeping a keen eye, however, upon the course of events. It is probable that the wily premier thought he could keep the young king in that subordinate position, but in this expectation he was greatly mistaken.

Akbar was destined to make his long reign as illustrious in the annals of Indian history as is that of his contemporary, Queen Elizabeth, in the history of England. He suddenly seized the reins of power, and issued an edict that only orders signed by his own hand were thenceforth to be obeyed. The enraged premier at first rebelled, but was subdued and pardoned, and, at his own request, was allowed to set out on a pilgrimage to Mecca, the holy shrine of faithful Mahomedans. But he was pursued by an Afghan, whose father he had caused to be put to death, and murdered before he could get away from India. Akbar then set himself to face the situation, and study the best means to attach his Hindoo subjects to his person and dynasty.

It was a gigantic subject to consider. The Hindoos of the north-west were in a tolerable degree of subjection and satisfaction with the Mogul government. They had found it, on the whole, more endurable than that of the early Mahomedan rulers, and were content to accept situations in its military and civil services, and be faithful subjects as long as there should be no other way open. But in the Deccan and Rajpootana it was very different. There were numerous small Hindoo kingdoms all over these territories, whose male population were almost wholly warriors. These warlike people could not be as easily subjugated as was the little kingdom of Gurrah and other aboriginal tribes, and when subjugated could not be depended upon to furnish happy and peaceable citizens. Akbar resolved to try diplomacy, and see if he could not attach some of the warlike Rajputs to him by the ties of marriage. He therefore sent messengers to visit the Rajpootana chieftains, and to ascertain where there were marriageable young ladies for whose hands he might sue. The result of all this planning and negotiation was, that Akbar received two Hindoo princesses in marriage—one of them the daughter of the Raja of Jodhpore, and the other the daughter of the Raja of Jeypore. The latter princess, Jodh Baie, was to be the queen elect, and her son the successor on the throne. These Hindoo Rajas evidently did not think enough of their faith to sacrifice their worldly prospects for it. Nothing could be further from the spirit of Hindooism than to allow the daughter of a pure twice-born Brahmin to wed with an outcast, which, according to their belief, all people, even kings, are, if not Hindoos. But the Hindoos are not blind to material advantages, and can even sacrifice religious scruples to gain them.

Of course, they knew that to refuse the offered alliance would be to bring the Mogul army at once upon them, which would soon take from them every vestige of feudal independence. They, therefore, made a virtue of necessity, and with as good a grace as possible consented to be honored by an alliance with the imperial power.

No further mention is made in history of the daughter of the Jodhpore Raja; but Jodh Baie, as mother of Jahangeer, the successor of Akbar, has honorable mention. It is recorded of her that she was of a particularly amiable and affectionate disposition, and remarkably free from bigotry; and such was her intelligence in matters of State, that the great Akbar did not disdain to seek her counsel, and often to be governed by it. It seems a strange anomaly, indeed, that the closely-indoctrinated daughter of a haughty Hindoo prince should become the wife and companion of the free-thinking and all-powerful Mogul king, and that he should give her so honorable a place in his affections and counsels. It is evident that the Moguls had greater respect for women than had the Mahomedans at that time, although not more, perhaps, than the Hindoos. However that may have been, the Sultana Jodh Baie was an acknowledged power in the land, and the Hindoo subjects of Akbar were drawn, through her influence, much closer to him than they would otherwise have been.

The legislation of Akbar was of a wise, protective kind, and the Hindoos were not slow to attribute the protection and favor they enjoyed to the influence of the good queen.

It is recorded by Hindoostanee writers that, some months after the arrival of Jodh Baie in the king's seraglio, she accompanied him on a pilgrimage to the city of Ajmere. The object of this journey was to visit the shrine of a celebrated moulvai, or priest, in order to gain some assurance in regard to the birth of a son who should be his successor.

The royal pair walked the whole distance of about two hundred miles in stages of six miles a day. Carpets were spread the whole distance for the queen to walk upon, so that her feet should not be injured. It would be sad, indeed, for a Hindoo lady of high rank to injure her feet, for they are colored, ringed, and cared for as tenderly as are her hands.

The sultana could then walk pleasantly along her carpeted way, untouched by the dust of the road, and untroubled by observation, for there were kanats, or cloth walls, erected on either side, so that her seclusion as a purdah-nisheen, or vailed lady, should not be violated. But even with all these comforts the daily walk of six miles must have been rather violent exercise for the high-born eastern lady, and one cannot help surmising that a palanquin and bearers were smuggled into the inclosure which assisted the royal progress. However, in *some* way the pilgrimage was completed, and high towers were built at the rest-houses where the royal *côrtege* halted each night.

In due time Akbar consulted the oracle in regard to the matter upon his mind, and in answer the priest, it is said, appeared to the king in a dream, and directed him to return to Agra, and to visit a priest of great sanctity, called Sheik Suleem, who lived twenty-two miles from Agra, at a place called Futte-pore-Seekree. They performed this journey likewise, and presented themselves before the priest, who predicted that a son would surely be born to them, who would live to a good old age, and would attain to great honor and glory. The king was greatly delighted at this prophecy, and desired the priest to take up his abode in the royal palace in Agra, and to become his confidential adviser; but he declined these flattering proposals, and expressed his determination to live and die in Futtepore-Seekree.

Akbar then resolved to remain in the same place, and to remove his court there. He at once began to arrange for mosques and palaces to be erected, and the hitherto quiet hamlet became suddenly a theater of royal display and splendor.

Within a year the Sultana Jodh Baie gave birth to a son, to whom they gave the name of the priest "Suleem," as a token of their gratitude. This name was borne by the prince thirty-five years, until he was raised to the throne with the title of Jahangeer, or "Conqueror of the World."

There are still many remains of the palaces and mosques that were erected in honor of the birth of Prince Suleem. They are situated within a walled inclosure which is seven miles in circumference, embracing the two villages of Futtepore and Seekree. Nearly in the center of this inclosure is a huge rock more than a mile in length. The buildings were very handsome, and were built in a very substantial manner of red sandstone and marble. On one of the principal gateways is the following inscription from the sacred traditions of the Mahomedans: "Said Jesus, on whom be peace, the world is a bridge; pass over it, but build no house there; he who hopeth for an hour may hope for an eternity; the world is but an hour, spend it in devotion."

After a few years it became evident that Futtepore-Seekree would never be popular as the Mogul capital, and Akbar removed the royal residence again to Agra. His Court was at this time most brilliant. He affected great liberality of views in religious matters, and welcomed learned men to his Court for the purpose of discussion. Among these were several Englishmen and Europeans; and there are reliable and very interesting statements from them in regard to the customs and manners of the Mogul nobility. The following paragraph gives a description of the personal appearance of Akbar:—

"The door of the khwabgah (place of dreams, that is, bed-chamber) opens, the large drums thunder from the naubat-khnana (royal orchestra) over the great doorway of the palace. A nakib issues forth, mace in hand, and proclaims in the monotonous tone so familiar to dwellers in the East the titles of his master. Immediately after him appears in the doorway a broad-chested man of some what advanced years. He is simply dressed, but there is a certain chasteness in the simplicity which shows that some little care has been taken to produce it. The material is white muslin, but gold thread is introduced in many parts with a very tasteful effect. You remark his arms as they are unusually long, his face is very clear, and the color of the blood so discernible as to give a rich tinge to his olive complexion; his eyebrows are joined and lowering, which tends to give a severe expression to the excessively bright eyes which they half conceal. This is Akbar. His appearance is the signal for a loud and general cry of 'Allah-oo-Akbar,' 'God is great;' to which the king, standing still in the doorway, and bowing slightly, responds, 'Jilli Jallalihoo,' 'his majesty is glorious.' This form of salutation and answer was originated by Akbar."

True to his policy, Akbar studied the Sanscrit language, and paid great attention to Hindoo literature. He interfered with none of the rites of their faith, except the cruel practices that had corrupted it. He forbade trials by ordeals, and the slaughter of animals for sacrifice; also the marriages of children. He sternly prohibited Suttee, or widow-burning, and allowed Hindoo widows to remarry. On one occasion hearing that his father-in-law, the Raja of Jodhpore, was about to force his son's widow to burn on the funeral pile of her husband, he personally interfered, and prevented the consummation of the deed.

He also put a stop to the practice of enslaving captives taken in war. Almost the only innovations upon religious customs which he made were in the interests of humanity, and his magnanimous policy, if carried out by his successors, would have wrought a great change in the country.

But it was left to a *Christian* Government to banish the cruelties of heathenism from the land of the Hindoos, and to educate the people in the principles of philanthropy.

There are no further memoirs of Jodh Baie except that upon her death—the exact date of which is not known—Akbar issued an edict that the court should go into mourning, and that the officers of the army, Hindoo as well as Mahomedan, should shave the mustache and beard. To make the matter sure, the royal barbers were to execute this mandate. All went on well until they came to the quarters of Rao Bhoy, the chief of the tribe of Hara, an inferior caste of Hindoos who were excellent warriors, and had been in this capacity of great assistance to

Akbar. There they were repulsed with threats. This rebellion was reported to Akbar, who was much incensed at the intelligence, and forgetting for the moment the great services rendered him by the chief recusant, ordered that he should be pinioned and shaved by force. "But," says the historian, "the barbers might as well have attempted to shave a tiger!" The Haras—as they were called—hastened to arm themselves, and there would soon have been bloodshed to commemorate the death of Jodh Baie had not the king repented of his folly and hastened to restore peace. He rode on his elephant to the camp, and, alighting, sought the incensed chieftain, and with words of praise and affection sought to calm his perturbed spirit. Rao Bhoy was glad to be conciliated, for he was strongly attached to the king. With true oriental adroitness he excused himself from obeying the mandate by saying, "An eater of pork, like me, is unworthy to put his lip in mourning for the queen!" As Mahomedans hate swine's flesh, and high-caste Hindoos abhor all meats, this excuse was very plausible. Akbar was delighted to have even so much of an acknowledgment as this, and, embracing the Rao, carried him off on his elephant, as was his wont, to the royal grounds.

Akbar erected a beautiful mausoleum over the remains of Jodh Baie, which was to be seen in Agra until about thirty years ago. It was then destroyed on account of some improvements for the military, by order of the British Government, greatly to the regret of the antiquary and all those interested in Indian history, and the memorials of that particularly interesting period in it when the Mogul dynasty was in power.

CHAND SULTANA,

A Chapter of Mogul History.

THE reign of Akbar, although one of great prosperity and brilliancy within its own bounds, did not carry peace and assurance to his neighbors.

Two of the most powerful Hindoo princes had become bound to him by the ties of marriage, and a few others being favorably inclined were allowed to become allies, but all of the remaining powers were under ban.

In 1568 the Mogul king set out on an expedition against the city of Chitore, whose ruler had grievously offended him. This city, which was taken from the Hindoos by the Mahomedans in 1303, when the dreadful tragedy detailed in our second chapter was enacted, had been re-occupied by the Hindoos for a long time.

Akbar was provided with a powerful force of artillery, and laid siege to the city in a very scientific manner. The Raja had fled to the hills and left his capital to be defended by Raja Jaimul, the brave Rajpoot chief of Bednore, who he probably thought would manage better than his own cowardly, inefficient self.

The siege was protracted for some time, until at

length the gallant Raja, while inspecting his ramparts, was slain by an arrow from the bow of Akbar himself. Upon his death the garrison lost all courage, and resolved to end their suspense by quick and entire destruction. Animated, probably, by a desire to emulate the bravery of their fathers, they built an immense funeral pyre for the body of the slain Raja, and caused all their women to throw themselves into the flames. The men then rushed out upon the Moguls and fought with desperation until every one was slain. Thus was re-enacted the fearful tragedy that had thrilled India about two and a half centuries before, but this time the city fell never to rise again. It was wrested forever from Hindoo ownership. The people were rich and prosperous when the Mogul army, like a mighty flood, came pouring in upon them, and Akbar estimated the weight of the golden ornaments that were taken from the bodies that were found, at seventy-four and a half mans, or five thousand nine hundred and sixty pounds; therefore Hindoos have ever since held the numerals 74½ as accursed. It seems strange that *men* should be so laden with ornament; but then, as now, it was the custom of the people, both male and female, to lay their extra money by in this way. As they have never had savings banks, this is almost the only way they can lay a little money by for a rainy day. This custom prevails at the present day; and it is not an uncommon thing to see laboring men with gold earrings and silver necklet and armlets, while the women have their nose-jewels and ear-drops, and neck, arms, fingers, toes, and ancles laden with jewelry.

The provinces of Guzerat, Bengal, .Sinde, and Candahar fell into the hands of Akbar during the conflicts and campaigns of the next twenty-five years, and in 1594 he found himself master of all his hereditary possessions, and all the country north of the Deccan that had ever belonged to the kingdom of Delhi. To the country south of the Nerbudda he then turned his attention and his forces, with the desire of adding the rich and populous provinces of the south country to his already overgrown and unwieldy empire.

In 1595 he seized an opening made by the rivalries consequent upon the throne of Ahmadnugger, being left vacant by the death of the king, to invade that city. Before his army reached Ahmadnugger, however, the throne had been given to Bahadur Nizam Shah, a child, and his aunt, Chand Sultana, had assumed the regency. This lady was a princess of Ahmadnugger, and had been married to the ruler of Beejapore in 1564; but he died in a few years, and she had returned, a widow, to her native city. She now found herself placed in a position of great responsibility and danger. She was surrounded by rival factions, all so eager in their private quarrels that they gave no heed to the Mogul army that, under the command of Prince Morad, the son of Akbar, was advancing upon Ahmadnugger. The sultana alone was awake to the danger. She knew that, single-handed, she could not cope with the Moguls, but that she and all the rebellious subjects together would fall an easy prey into their hands. She, therefore, sought, with all her woman's tact and power of persuasion, to have the leaders of the feuds become reconciled to each other, and to combine their energies against the common enemy. In this effort she was successful, and the nobility and the common people joined together as one man in preparations to defend their capital.

The Moguls advanced and laid siege to the city, and began to construct mines under the walls. Two of these were discovered, and through the strict vigilance of the sultana, and in obedience to her orders, were rendered harmless; but a third one was not discovered, and blew up, making a large breach in the wall. Upon this disaster some of the officers supposed all was over, and prepared to desert the defense and make good their escape. But the sultana hastened to the spot in full armor with a drawn sword in her hand. It is recorded, however, that, even in this extremity, she wore a vail to hide her face from the gaze of the soldiery.

Her brave, undaunted demeanor inspired some of the troops with courage, and others with shame. All rallied to the defense of the breach. Guns were quickly brought into position to bear upon it, and deal death among the Moguls who were striving to rush through into the city. Rockets, gunpowder, and combustibles of every kind that could be laid hold of were thrown among the besiegers. The contest became sharp and bloody. Prince Morad, at the head of his fierce Moguls, was determined not to lose the opportunity to get into the city; while the heroic sultana and her troops were fighting for life, and all that makes life dear. It is affirmed by native historians, that, upon the supply of shot becoming exhausted, the sultana gave orders for the treasury to be opened, and the coin to be used in loading the guns. First the copper was used, then the silver, and, finally, gold mohurs and jewels flashed along in brilliant, but deadly, lines upon the enemy.

At length, as night closed in, the Moguls were obliged to retire, and the besieged city was left for a few hours to repose. Of course this lull was taken advantage of by the brave queen and her now enthusiastic soldiers. They had actually resisted the Moguls successfully *once*, and might do so again, and always; so with strong hearts and hands they set to work to repair the breach in the wall of the city. The sultana herself superintended the work, and by morning it was accomplished. Outside help also appeared with the morning light. Some neighboring tribes, to whom the sultana had applied for aid, had sent troops to her assistance, and as the blue mist lifted they were descried in the distance.

The Moguls saw the breach was repaired, and that re-enforcements were approaching. They were without provisions, and their valor was consequently diminished ; therefore they made proposals of peace, and offered to retire if Chand Sultāna would cede the province of Berar to the Mogul king.

The sultana had little confidence in the continuation of the enthusiasm and courage which then animated her troops, and which her own heroism had roused. She, therefore, thought it wise and prudent to accede to the proposed terms of peace. So the Mogul army was withstood, and the threatened danger for the time averted, by the courage and heroism of a woman.

Encouraged by this successful stemming of the stream of Mogul power that they had feared must soon overwhelm them, the rulers of Ahmadnugger, Beejapore, and Golconda formed an alliance to drive the Mogul army over the Nerbudda river back to their own territories. They brought an army of sixty thousand men into the field, and attacked the Moguls, but after two days' sharp fighting no decisive result was reached, as both parties claimed the victory. The Mogul army was crippled, however, and, although not beaten back, found itself unable to carry on the work-of conquest ; and Akbar, becoming impatient, proceeded in person to the Deccan.

Immediately upon his arrival he sent an army to besiege Ahmadnugger and its brave queen. The poor sultana was at this time in the midst of greater internal discords than before. She was literally surrounded by enemies who were eager to break the Government up, hoping in the general confusion that would ensue in some way to aggrandize themselves.

The sultana, understanding perfectly the faithlessness of her own people and of the neighboring princes, endeavored to make terms with the Moguls, and would probably have succeeded had not some of her soldiers, instigated by her enemies, broken into the women's apartments and put her to death.

So the noble, heroic woman met a violent death at last!

What a cruel thing is love of conquest, it holds human life at so low a rate when it stands in the way of success in cherished schemes! It would seem that Akbar might have been content with Northern Hindoostan, and not have coveted the little kingdom ruled by a brave but unfortunate woman; but even if he had been so magnanimous, it is in no wise certain that Chand Sultana would have been suffered to reign unmolested. In those warlike times war was the rule and peace the exception, and was never enjoyed by a kingdom for any length of time unless it was stronger than its neighbors. *Chand* is the Hindoostanee name for *moon*, and it may be said that the clear moonlight of Chand Sultana's prosperity paled and disappeared before the blazing sun of Akbar's glory! But her destruction did not prove an occasion of good fortune to her home enemies. The Mogul army gave no quarter, but plundered the city and murdered all who withstood them; and the young king, the nephew of Chand Sultana, was sent with his family as a State prisoner to the city of Gwalior. This occurred in 1600, four years after the heroic and successful resistance made to the Mogul army by Chand Sultana.

This was almost the final act of importance during the reign of Akbar. The close of his life was rendered unhappy by the impatience of Prince Suleem to take his position as king. He even went so far as to take up arms against his father, but a kind paternal letter made him lay them down again and resolve to wait his appointed time. But his conduct had so alienated a large body of the nobility who were deeply attached to the king, that when Akbar was near to death they tried to persuade him to appoint the son of Suleem, Prince Khushroo, to the throne. But the king could not be swerved from his purpose. He called for Prince Suleem, his beloved son, who was, he believed, given to him in answer to prayer, and made him bind the royal scimetar on his side, as a token that the kingdom was bequeathed to him. He then recommended his people, personal friends, and the women of his zenana, to his protection; and after asking pardon of all around for any offense he might have committed against them, repeated the Mahomedan confession of faith, and died. His death occurred the thirteenth of October, 1605, in the sixty-second year of his age and forty-ninth of his reign; and "Akbar the Great" fell into the ranks of the past, and Suleem his son reigned in his stead.

According to Marshman "Akbar was not only the ornament of the Mogul dynasty, but incomparably the greatest of all the Mahomedan rulers of India. Few princes ever exhibited greater military genius or personal courage. He never fought a battle which he did not win, or besieged a town which he did not take, yet he had no passion for war; and as soon as he had turned the tide of victory by his skill and energy, he was happy to have his generals complete his work, and to hasten back to the more agreeable labors of the cabinet."

Akbar's religious opinions were far from being fixed. Like Pilate, his inquiry was, "What is truth?" and he seemed to sincerely wish to know it. In early life he was a zealous, though not bigoted, Mahomedan; but when about twenty-five years old his views became very liberal, and he rejected all prophets, priests, and religious ceremonies, professing to take reason as his only guide.

It is supposed he had some idea of founding a liberal religion, one that would embrace people of widely different views and practices. He caused the formula "There is no God but one, and *Akbar* is his prophet," to be proclaimed throughout his dominions. This creed certainly abolished *Mahomed.* But when Akbar came to his last hours, and felt the weakness of dissolution stealing upon him, he seems to have been more humble than he was when at the zenith of worldly prosperity, and to have wished to give back to Mahomed the dignity of which he had sought to rob him, by confessing with his last breath, "There is but one God, and *Mahomed* is his prophet."

In spite of his heterodox religious opinions, Akbar was greatly beloved both by Mahomedans and Hindoos. They all enjoyed toleration alike, and alike shared the royal favor. All Akbar required of his people was loyalty to the Government and honorable dealing among themselves. He desired to have his position secure by its being founded upon the love and confidence of his subjects, of whatever creed or standing. There were no religious tests to fit men for office, but "neutrality in religion and protection for all," was his motto.

The tomb of Akbar is at Sikundra, about six miles from Agra. It was built by his son and successor, who took so much interest in having it worthy of a distinguished ruler and an indulgent father, that, not being pleased with its appearance when nearly completed, he had it torn down, and rebuilt at an added expense of fifteen lacs of rupees, or seven hundred and fifty thousand dollars. It is an elaborate structure of sandstone and marble.

The tomb which contains the royal dust is in a vaulted hall on the ground floor, and on the summit of the building, surrounded by a beautiful screen of marble network, is the upper tomb, under a canopy of white marble surmounted by a gilded dome. Upon it the ninety-nine names which are ascribed to God by Mahomedans are sculptured, in Arabic characters. Near by is another structure, said to be the tomb of Miriam, a Portuguese wife of Akbar, and a Roman Catholic. Not much is known of this lady, but it seems certain that there was such an inmate of the royal seraglio. Her mausoleum is now used for the printing-press of the Anglican Church Mission. Our delightful poet, Whittier, founded his poem of "Miriam" upon this item of history, and I cannot forbear to make a quotation from it in bidding farewell to Akbar, the Great Mogul:—

"Two leagues from Agra still the traveler sees
The tomb of Akbar through its cypress trees;
And near at hand the marble walls that hide
The Christian Begum sleeping at his side:
And o'er her vault of burial (who shall tell
If it be chance alone, or miracle?)
The *Mission Press* with tireless hands unrolls
The words of Jesus on its lettered scrolls;
Tells in all tongues the tale of mercy o'er,
And bids the guilty 'Go, and sin no more.'"

Noor Mahal.

NOOR MAHAL,

The Light of the Palace—A Chapter of Mogul History.

WHO has not heard of Noor Mahal the beautiful, the "Light of the Palace," or Noor Jahan, as she was often called, that is, the "Light of the World," the chosen above the most lovely of the Mogul seraglio? who was raised to the highest rank by the fascination of her wonderful beauty, and retained it by her talent and force of character.

Of her personal charms Moore wrote:—

> "That loveliness ever in motion, which plays
> Like the light upon Autumn's soft, shadowy days;
> Now here and now there, giving warmth as it flies
> From the lip to the cheek, from the cheek to the eyes;
> Now melting in mist, and now breaking in gleams,
> Like the glimpses a saint hath of heaven in his dreams."

And it is evident that the charms of her mind were quite as superior as those of her person, for it was not till the latter had become dimmed by her approach to middle life that she became the wife of Jehangeer, the "Conqueror of the World," who, when Prince Suleem, became so deeply attached to her that his affection lasted as long as his life.

This lady, whose career was so singularly fortunate —in a worldly sense—was, in her infancy, dependent upon charity for her very existence. Her ancestors were of good family in Teheran, in Persia; but her father, although a man of talent, was reduced to poverty, and resolved to emigrate to India, hoping to better his fortunes in the service of the "Great Mogul." A Persian merchant was about this time starting off with a caravan of merchandise for the Court of Akbar, and Mirza Ghaias, the father of Noor Mahal, obtained permission to travel in their company. It was not safe for families to travel alone through the mountain passes and plains, with their half-savage inhabitants, in those days, and travelers always availed themselves of the protection afforded by the caravan that yearly carried the products of Persian fields and Persian skill to the Mogul capital and the chief cities of Northern India.

The family of Mirza Ghaias consisted of his wife and one son, and shortly after they began their journey a little delicate daughter was born. The young stranger, who was destined to be for many years the Sultana of India, was of such beautiful form and feature as to excite the admiration of every one who beheld her; but the father, unmoved by her beauty, declared that he could not be burdened with her, and placed her by the roadside, either to perish or be rescued by some man to whom providence had bequeathed larger worldly possessions than to himself. The wealthy owner of the caravan saw the lovely infant, and (as the father quite probably expected) inquired into the matter. The family and their long-continued misfortunes were thus brought to his notice. He was favorably impressed by the father's account of himself, and promised to befriend him and recommend him to Akbar. The little babe was to be reared and educated with great care, wholly at the merchant's expense. Meanwhile she was consigned to her mother's arms again, having, by her brief absence, accomplished a total change in the prospects and fortunes of the whole family. We can imagine, however, that the mother's joy at recovering her lost treasure exceeded that she experienced in prospect of better fortunes.

How wonderful are the ways of Providence, and with what insignificant means God can work out great results! Prince Suleem, the future ruler of India, was a man given over to the indulgence of all the baser passions of his nature; but Noor Mahal, the queen and helpmeet whom God raised up for him, rescued him from sinking into the depths of sensuality and cruelty, and stood, like an angel of mercy, between him and the people.

The caravan journeyed on toward the plains of Hindoostan. We can fancy the long train of heavily-laden camels as it drags its slow length along over the sandy plains and across the shallow rivers, through the months of the dry, cold season, when the widest rivers shrink to brooks; stopping sometimes at night in the spacious court-yards surrounded by little rooms forming the caravanserai, or hotel for caravans; and again when, far from any such place of safety, camping out in the open air, and depending upon their own armed band and fierce watch-dogs for safe-keeping. At last they reached Agra, the Mogul capital at that time, and the kind merchant, according to his promise, spoke so highly in praise of Mirza Ghaias that a position of trust and emolument in the service of Akbar was given to him.

Once installed in a place suited to his talents, Mirza Ghaias soon rose to eminence, and became noted for his excellent sense in matters of State, and for his uncommon honesty. Akbar was delighted at the acquisition he had made, for men of acuteness and integrity were as scarce at the Mogul Court as at most courts, and in a few years the poor, despairing adventurer became the most respected and trusted of all the nobles at the Court of Akbar.

The mother of Noor Mahal was a clever woman of cultivated intellect and manners. Like many Persian ladies, she was skilled in the preparation and uses of perfumes and cosmetics. It is said that she introduced the famous attar of roses into India, and taught a very few favored ones how to distill it. This delicious perfume is made from the fragrant Bussorah roses. In Persia and Cashmere large fields of roses are cultivated for the manufacture of attar, and also of rose water.

Probably her skill in these delicate matters was the reason why the mother of Noor Mahal was asked to visit the royal zenana, within the walls of the fort of Agra. She became a great favorite with the lonely prisoners, who, even in gilded cages, found time often lag heavily, and, with her young and exquisitely beautiful daughter, always received a warm welcome.

Noor Mahal was blooming into rare beauty, and it is no wonder that she captivated the young heir-apparent, Prince Suleem, whom she often met in his mother's apartments. As years went on and the children were fast ripening into maturity, the watchful mother of Noor Mahal became alarmed for her child. She could not expect that Akbar would allow the prince to marry Noor Mahal, and she was resolved that the beauty of her only and cherished daughter should not prove the cause of her ruin. She, therefore, spoke to the sultana, Jodh Baie, in regard to the attachment springing up between her daughter and prince Suleem, and expressed her desire to remove her child from court. The sultana promised to speak to Akbar on the subject, and shortly after did so. The king was alarmed, and, calling the prince, explained to him that he must choose his wives from political reasons, and begged him to give up all thought of the beautiful young Persian. The prince promised to obey, but Akbar thought best to make the matter sure by marrying Noor Mahal to some one else. A fine young man, called Sher Afghan, had long been proposing for her hand. It is said the name Sher was given him because he had once killed a tiger—a sher—single-handed. Upon him, therefore, her hand was bestowed, and Akbar presented them with a jageer or estate in Bengal, and the young couple departed for their distant home.

Years passed on, Akbar slept with his fathers, and Prince Suleem was crowned king of India, with the title of Jahangeer, or "Conqueror of the World."

It soon became evident that time had not weakened the affection felt by Prince Suleem for the object of his boyhood's love. After he had reigned about a year he sent his foster brother, Kutub-oo-Deen, as Viceroy to Bengal, and charged him in some way to get possession of Noor Mahal, and to send her, under the protection of an escort, to Agra. The line of policy was to bribe Sher Afghan, by preferment, to give his wife up to the king; but, suspecting their designs, he refused to act as an officer of government, and signified that he did not consider himself in the service of the Mogul king by leaving off the wearing of arms. The Viceroy persisted in his proposals, now openly made, and backed them with threats. The high-spirited but imprudent husband became indignant, and then furious, and attempted to murder the Viceroy. Perhaps he was purposely provoked to this, in order to give color to the high-handed measures intended to be taken against him. However this may have been, he was slain, and Noor Mahal was forwarded to the court at Agra.

It is supposed that she had become sincerely attached to her husband, and deeply resented his foul murder. From this or some other cause the marriage, so ardently longed for by Jehangeer, did not take place until four years after the death of Sher Afghan. Noor Mahal was then thirty-four years of age, and the king was forty-three. It was supposed that Jehangeer was very unhappy during this long separation. It was this estrangement that formed the basis of Moore's beautiful poem, "The Light of the Harem," in "Lalla Rookh." The following lines bear especial reference to it:—

"Alas, how light a cause may move
Dissension between hearts that love!
Hearts that the world in vain had tried,
And sorrow but more closely tied;
That stood the storm, when waves were rough,
Yet in a sunny hour fall off,
Like ships that have gone down at sea
When heaven was all tranquillity!
A something light as air—a look,
  A word unkind, or wrongly taken,
O! love that tempests never shook,
  A breath, a touch like this hath shaken.
And ruder words will soon rush in
To spread the breach that words begin;
And eyes forget the gentle ray
They wore in courtship's smiling day;
And voices lose the tone that shed
A tenderness round all they said;
Till, fast declining, one by one
The sweetnesses of love are gone;
And hearts so lately mingled, seem
Like broken clouds, or like the stream

That, smiling, left the mountain's brow
As though its waters ne'er could sever,
Yet, ere it reach the plain below,
Breaks into floods that part forever."

But with all their pathos and beauty, these lines are not at all suited to the case. It was no "slight cause" that angered Noor Mahal, and kept her so long from occupying the lofty position waiting for her acceptance.

The following six lines are probably more just in their application. They represent Jahangeer at the feast of roses in the valley of Cashmere, where the Mogul Court often removed during the hot season :—

"In vain the valley's smiling throng
Worship him as he moves along ;
He heeds them not —one smile of hers
Is worth a world of worshipers.
They but the stars' adorers are ;
She is the heaven that lights the star !"

The following lines, also, are too beautiful to omit from these pages, especially as the last two are actually inscribed over the entrance to a magnificent audience hall which yet stands in Delhi. They are the first words with which Noor Mahal tried her enchanted harp and voice in order to win back her Selim's love :—

"There's a bliss beyond all that the minstrel has told,
When two that are linked in one heavenly tie,
With heart never changing, and brow never cold,
Love on through all ills, and love on till they die !

One hour of a passion so sacred is worth
  Whole ages of heartless and wandering bliss;
And, O! if there *be* an *Elysium* on earth,
  It is this, it is this!"

At length, after four years of widowhood and just resentment, Noor Mahal began to think more favorably of her royal suitor, and contrived to place herself where they would meet. The king was quick to perceive the change in her feelings, and renewed his proposals with ardor. Their marriage was celebrated with great pomp and rejoicings, and the king delighted then, and ever after, to crown his long-loved queen with all the honors at his command. Thenceforward her life was closely interwoven with his, and her influence quite as great as his in the kingdom, because she influenced *him* in every thing. He associated her name with his upon the coin of the realm, an honor never before bestowed by any king of India upon his queen; and consulted her upon State questions and all the details of Court politics. For her sake he even denied himself the pleasure of continual inebriation, and made a point of remaining sober until the business of the day was finished. This course, no doubt, added considerably to the dignity of the Court. She exercised her influence, also, to soften the cruel, vindictive disposition of the king, and through her intercessions many poor, weak culprits, more sinned against than sinning, escaped undue punishment for their foolish complicity with mischievous and intriguing political agitators.

The Court, under the loose control of Jahangeer, had during the five years of his reign very much deteriorated. Instead of the learned professors and theological discussions of the times of Akbar, the disciples of Bacchus had full sway under Jahangeer. Day and night the red wine flowed, and hilarity and buffoonery filled the flying hours ; but with all this dissipation there were a few men, with the king at their head, who had brains and determination enough to give a little time to business and to keep the wheels of State in motion. Jahangeer's cruel vengeance was also dreaded by all malcontents, and altogether matters went on more favorably than would seem possible under such a *régime*. With the entrance of Noor Mahal into this mad, frolicsome Court came many changes for the better, not suddenly and violently made, but gradually and gracefully, so that the added splendor imparted by her taste satisfied the craving for magnificence so prevalent among Orientals, and compensated them for the loss of the glare and flare of barbaric and vulgar gayety. Her father, Mirza Ghaias, who had long been one of the most honored and faithful ministers of the Mogul Court, was now placed at the head of affairs as vizier, or prime minister, and her brother, Asof Khan, was also raised to a position and rank befitting the brother of the queen.

One of the many accomplishments of Noor Mahal, and which was particularly captivating to Jahangeer, is said to have been her facility in composing extemporaneous verses. Her courage and masculine tastes also pleased him, and he used to boast that on a hunting party she killed four tigers, with a matchlock, from her elephant. In every respect she seemed to be the woman of all others fitted to occupy the position she held. The king was reported to have said, "Before I married *her* I never knew what marriage really meant." Her name originally was Mihr-ul-Nissa, that is, "the Lady of Mercy," and was, quite likely, given her by her parents in token of the kind charity of the merchant who succored her, and became in consequence the benefactor of the whole family; but it is noteworthy that she really was what her first name implies, a kind and considerate benefactor of the needy. She became the especial patroness of orphan girls, it is said, and gave marriage portions out of her own funds to several hundred girls who were left without their natural protectors.

From the time of her marriage, Noor Mahal mixed so much in public affairs that it would be impossible to sketch her life without also giving the main events connected with the reign of Jahangeer.

There were four sons of Jahangeer's who reached mature age. Prince Khushroo, the eldest, the legitimate heir to the throne, forfeited his right by listening to bad advisers, and allowing himself to be put forward in place of his father when Akbar, his grandfather, lay at the point of death.

Jahangeer, however, pardoned his son, in consideration of his youth and inexperience; but after his accession the foolish prince again appeared in array against his father, and headed a band of rebellious soldiers in attacking the regular army. He was defeated, and was sentenced to be kept in perpetual confinement, as too turbulent a spirit to be allowed to run at large.

Purvez, the second son, was a good soldier, but lacked mental ability, and on this account was not thought worthy to succeed to so responsible a position. Prince Khurrum, the third son, was a fine character. His mother was a Hindoo, a Rajpootnee, of the same tribe as the Hindoo wife of Akbar and her namesake as well, and her son possessed in a marked degree the manly qualities peculiar to the Rajputs, and was celebrated also for his fine taste in art, and his good sense. He was married to Mumtaz Mahal, the niece of Noor Mahal, and daughter of Asof Khan, and, of course, the influence of Noor Mahal was all in his favor. He early distinguished himself as an able general, and was greatly valued by his father for his usefulness in this capacity; for Jahangeer had by this time become a confirmed invalid through his reckless dissipation, and was quite unfit to take the field in person.

In 1612 Jahangeer sent an army into the Deccan against Malik Ambar, but it was entirely defeated. A second army, that was sent to re-enforce the first, arrived too late, and joined with it in retracing their steps across the Nerbudda.

In 1614 the Moguls were more successful in arms against the Hindoos, and, with Prince Khurrum at their head, completely overcame the Rana of Oodipore, and compelled him to promise allegiance to the Mogul king; but the prince remembered that his mother was a Hindoo princess, and restored to the Rana all his territories, retaining him, however, as a vassal of the Mogul Government.

In 1615, the tenth year of the reign of Jahangeer, James I. of England sent an embassador to the Mogul Court to arrange certain matters pertaining to the rights and privileges of the East India Company, then newly established in a few of the seaport towns. Sir Thomas Roe was the name of the embassador. He traveled in various parts of the Mogul kingdom, and carefully noted every thing he saw. He was quite dazzled by the magnificence of the Mogul Court, but he formed a very low estimate in regard to the comfort of the common people and the discipline of the army.

In 1617 Jahangeer determined to send another expedition against Malik Ambar, and desired Prince Khurrum to take the command. The prince, knowing that his father's health was insecure, and that, in the event of his death, he ought to be on the ground to assert his claim to the throne, hesitated about accepting a charge that would take him away to so distant a part of the country. It should be borne in mind that there were no railroads then to almost annihilate distance. The king bestowed the title of Shah Jahan, or "King of the World," upon the prince at this juncture, as if to settle the question of heirship to the throne; but the prince still felt himself insecure, especially as Prince Khushroo had just been released through the mediation of Prince Purvez. At last he accepted the appointment, on condition that Prince Khushroo should be committed to his charge and accompany him on the expedition. This request was at once complied with, and the army and the royal brothers departed to the Deccan, and again invaded the territories of the indomitable and brave prince. For a long time the Moguls gained no permanent success, and Shah Jahan was obliged at last to descend to bribery in order to gain his ends. By extravagant offers he succeeded in corrupting several Mahratta Rajas in the army of Malik Ambar, and in 1621 defeated him in battle, and compelled him to purchase peace at a large sacrifice of treasure and territory.

About this time Jahangeer fell ill with asthma, and it was thought that his career was nearly ended. The news was carried to the army, shortly after which Prince Khushroo was murdered, Early one morning his wife entered his tent and found him weltering in his blood.

It was supposed at one time that this prince

might have regained the favor of his father through the influence of the all-powerful Noor Mahal, if he had acceded to her wish that he should marry her daughter by Sher Afghan; but he steadily refused her offers from affection for the wife to whom he had been for some time married. She urged him to accept the offer, and thus increase his chances of winning back his birthright; but he was not to be moved. She had been the patient and loving companion of his long captivity, and accompanied him on this journey to the south. No wonder that she filled the Mogul camp with her cries and lamentations when she found the lifeless body of her murdered husband, and refused to be comforted.

The foul deed was, of course, supposed to have been instigated by Shah Jahan, but it was never proved; and many believed him to be incapable of so great a crime. It certainly was not in keeping with his general character.

It would naturally be supposed that this event would have cleared away all the obstacles in Shah Jahan's path to the throne; but, strange to say, it proved to be the beginning of a long series of dangers and difficulties in his way.

It happened on this wise: Jahangeer partially recovered, and upon hearing of Prince Khushroo's violent death was suspicious of Shah Jahan, believing him to have been accessary to it. Noor Mahal had recently married her daughter to Prince Sheriar, the youngest son of the king, and her ambitious soul at once conceived the project of taking advantage of the king's displeasure toward Shah Jahan by advancing the interests of her son-in-law. She was, of course, by this time in love with power, and did not like to fall from the high position she had occupied so long and so well. It was evident that Shah Jahan would be sole master if he became king, but she might manage the younger and weaker prince, especially since he had become her son-in-law. The king's health continued in a very precarious state, and Noor Mahal decided to lose no time in beginning to undermine the influence of Shah Jahan.

At her instance the king asked him to now undertake the recovery of the distant province of Candahar, which had been seized by the Persians. He at first consented, and marched a short distance north with his army, but halted and demanded that some security should be given him before proceeding farther. This demand was skillfully represented to Jahangeer as an evidence of insubordination, and he at once ordered Shah Jahan to send the greater part of his army to the capital, that it might be put under the charge of Prince Sheriar, who would take command of the expedition to Candahar. The chief officers were ordered to proceed direct to Prince Sheriar's camp. Shah Jahan remonstrated, but was quickly ordered off to the Deccan. His estates in Hindoostan proper, that is, north of the Nerbudda, were transferred to Prince Sheriar, and he was told to select an equivalent in the Deccan or Guzerat.

About this time Mirza Ghaias, the father of Noor Mahal, died at an advanced age. He was a fine statesman and accomplished courtier to the last. It was said that just before he died the king went in to speak with him. The sultana was seated by her dying father, tenderly ministering to his wants. The aged man's eyes were so dim that he did not at once recognize his illustrious son-in-law. Noor Mahal asked, "Do you know, my father, who it is that is come to visit you?" He understood that it was the king, and, turning his eyes toward him, replied quickly, with true oriental exaggeration :—

> "If a blind man in thy presence happened to be standing now,
> Even he would surely know thee by the splendor of thy brow."

Asof Khan, the brother of the queen, became prime minister upon the death of their father, and as he was father-in-law to Shah Jahan, it is not surprising that he favored his pretensions. Noor Mahal, therefore, found herself in the minority, and resolved upon bold measures. She persuaded Jahangeer to send for Muhabbat Khan, a very able general, at that time governor of Cabul, and enlisted him on her side. The king meanwhile became convinced that Shah Jahan was trying to usurp his authority, and put several persons to death on suspicion of their complicity with him.

Shah Jahan saw that his father was quite turned against him, and, despairing of a peaceable settlement, resolved to fight for his throne.

Muhabbat Khan was placed in command of the king's army immediately, upon his arrival at the capital, and he proceeded at once against Shah Jahan. That prince, in spite of his determination to fight since forced to do so, did not manifest his usual skill in the action that ensued. The result was indecisive, and Shah Jahan retired, soon after the engagement, to the Deccan. If he looked for any help or sympathy in that quarter he soon learned to the contrary. The Hindoo kings, whom he had brought into subjection to the Mogul power, refused to give him any assistance. Many of his soldiers, thinking his cause a hopeless one, deserted, but he pressed on to Telingana, and, gathering some adventurous spirits as he marched, proceeded along the coast from Masulipatam northward, and took possession of the provinces of Bengal and Behar. He then marched upon Allahabad, where he was met by Muhabbat Khan. An action ensued in which Shah Jahan was defeated, and he again fled to the Deccan. This time he found a friend in Malik Ambar, who had fallen out with the king; but Muhabbat Khan had too many resources at his command to allow matters to go on in this way. He pressed Shah Jahan so fiercely that he was soon obliged to seek reconciliation with his father, and obtained it on condition of full surrender, and by giving two of his sons as hostages.

So the unnatural struggle ended, and matters were just about as they were before it began. Noor Mahal ascertained about this time that Muhabbat Khan was not favorable to the succession of Prince Sheriar to the throne, and she resolved to effect his removal if possible. She caused a charge of embezzlement to be brought against him, and he was summoned to Court to meet it. He came promptly, bringing five thousand Rajputs along to help him plead his cause if necessary.

He had, a little before this, betrothed his daughter to a young man of good family, without asking the king's consent, as was customary. This was reported to Jahangeer, who became furiously angry, and caused the young man to be stripped and whipped with thorns in the presence of the Court, and confiscated his property.

The king and his Court were marching to Cabul when Muhabbat Khan arrived to meet the charge against his integrity. Upon his arrival he proceeded to the royal encampment but was not allowed to enter, and in every way was made to understand that the sunshine of royal favor no longer shone upon him. He saw that his case was a desperate one, and resolved to take desperate measures. On the morning after his arrival the royal camp and army were to cross the river Hydaspes. Jahangeer had been considerably overcome with wine the previous evening, and did not move on with the army, but remained behind, with but a slender guard, to sleep off the effects of the night's dissipation. Muhabbat Khan saw his opportunity and improved it. Taking a small body of men, he surrounded the king's tent and made him prisoner. Jahangeer was overwhelmed with surprise and indignation, but, as there was no help for it, he allowed himself to be assisted upon an elephant, and, with his indispensable cup-bearer and goblet, was carried off to the camp of Muhabbat Khan.

Noor Mahal disguised herself hastily and made good her escape to the royal army across the river, where she at once summoned the officers to concert plans to rescue the king. The daring Rajputs destroyed the bridge over the Hydaspes, and the imperialists had no boats. They discovered a ford at a little distance, however, and soon began to march over with the queen at their head. She was armed, and mounted on a noble elephant. The Rajputs attacked them furiously while crossing, pouring showers of balls, rockets, and arrows upon the struggling masses as they were trying to effect their passage. Many were driven into the water. The guards of the queen were cut down, and she herself narrowly escaped. Her elephant was wounded, and its driver killed. The order to retreat was given, and the demoralized Moguls endeavored to recross the river.

The elephant of Noor Mahal, wounded, and deprived of the guiding hand of its driver, was carried down stream by the force of the current, and she was for awhile in great danger ; but she was carried safely to land at last, and when found by her terrified attendants was calmly dressing the wounds of her little grandson, who had been with her through the deadly fray, and had been wounded by arrows meant for her.

Finding herself outdone in the field, Noor Mahal went to the rebel camp to join her husband, and threw herself upon the mercy of Muhabbat Khan. They were both treated with great respect, but were held in strict captivity.

Muhabbat Khan took command of the royal army and crossed the Indus to Cabul, where they encamped. Noor Mahal had, by this time, a perfect understanding with the army through her skillful intrigues, and Muhabbat Khan felt that his position, and even his life, were very insecure. Noor Mahal offered him the royal pardon and favor if he would join her in putting Shah Jahan down and raising Sheriar, but the general did not like the idea of the feeble-minded Sheriar for the ostensible king, with Noor Mahal for the real ruler, and resolved to join Shah Jahan and uphold his claims to the throne. He accordingly drew his own troops off very suddenly and marched to Sinde, where Shah Jahan was waiting to watch the course of events. Noor Mahal was enraged at his desertion, and offered a large reward for his apprehension or murder; but her intrigues and schemes for vengeance were suddenly ended by the approach of a mightier king than those of earth. Death came and summoned the Mogul king to *his* court.

Jahangeer, in spite of his life of luxurious dissipation, lived to attain the age of sixty years. He died October 28, 1627. Marshman says of him: "He was contemporary with James the First of England. Not only were their reigns of the same duration, but there was a remarkable accordance in their characters. They were both equally weak and contemptible, both the slaves of favorites and of drink, and, by a singular coincidence, they both launched a royal decree against the use of tobacco, then recently introduced into England and India, and in both cases with the same degree of success." As the father-in-law of Shah Jahan was prime minister, and the greatest general of the realm was his friend, his way to the throne was now open. He at once took possession, and Noor Mahal, who for sixteen years had exercised so wide an influence in the kingdom, was now obliged to retire to the shades of private life. She was allowed a pension of twenty-five lakhs of rupees, or one and a quarter million dollars a year. It is probable that her daughter dwelt with her during these last years of her life, for her husband, the unfortunate Prince Sheriar, was put to death by order of Shah Jahan, no doubt by the advice of Muhabbat Khan. Noor Mahal lived in the city of Lahore, the capital of the province now called the Punjab, that is, the land of the five rivers, and busied herself in building a beautiful mausoleum for her royal husband. It is said that she never wore colors after the death of Jahangeer, but always dressed in pure white. She lived in comparative seclusion, winning the love and respect of all whom she mingled with by her virtues and charities. She lived nineteen years after the death of Jahangeer, and died at the age of sixty-nine, in the year 1646. She was buried by the side of her husband, and their tombs, in the beautiful edifice she had erected, are preserved with great care.

The mausoleum stands about three miles from the city of Lahore, in the midst of a delightful garden, rich in all the luxuriant splendor of oriental vegetation.

Another memorial of Noor Mahal is still in existence. It is the tomb of her father, Mirza Ghaias, or Itmad-oo-Dowlah, as he was entitled after he rose to eminence in the service of Jahangeer. It is in Agra, not very far from the famous Taj Mahal, in a beautiful garden which had probably belonged to his residence.

This memorial is inferior to the superb edifices erected by Shah Jahan, and looks coarse beside them. It is said that Noor Mahal wished to overlay it with silver, but was overruled by her architect, who represented to her the temptation it would be to the people.

The name of Noor Mahal is familiar to the inhabitants of Northern India to this day, and is to them a synonym for beauty and talent. Her likeness, in miniature, beautifully painted on ivory, has been preserved, and many copies have been made, from one of which the accompanying picture was engraved.

Mumtag Mahal.

MUMTAZ MAHAL.

A Chapter of Mogul History.

THE Moguls, in spite of their warlike propensities, were not devoid of culture, and the period of their rule in India was particularly favorable for poets and prose writers, whether novelists or historians. They were more luxurious and elegant in their tastes than the early Mahomedan rulers, and were from the beginning great patrons of science and literature.

The reign of Baber was so short that no great change was effected in the tastes of the people; that of Humayoon was so broken and disturbed that public tastes and morals rather retrograded than otherwise; but during the long prosperous reign of Akbar, and the shorter but as prosperous one of Jahangeer, science and literature flourished as they never had previously in Hindoostan.

The reign of Shah Jahan was equally beneficent and prosperous; while in the magnificence of his entertainments and his passion for splendid architecture he went quite beyond all his predecessors.

In 1628, a year after his accession to the throne, he was proclaimed king in the city of Agra, and on that occasion made a most gorgeous display of the wealth of the royal treasury. A suite of tents was manufactured of the finest Cashmere shawls, for royal occupation. He revived the ancient Hindoo custom of being weighed against gold, silver, and gems, which were afterward distributed among the courtiers. Vases were filled with gems and waved over his head, and then emptied on the floor for a general scramble. The expense of these festivities was estimated at seven and a half millions of dollars.

He was a liberal patron of poets, prose writers, and musicians, and left the impress of his genius and taste upon the face of the country as no other monarch has done.

The present city of Delhi was built by him, and was called Shahjahanabad, or the "City of Shah Jahan." It stands about five miles from the ruins of the old city, and is in a fair state of preservation in spite of the many sanguinary events which have transpired within its walls. The city has ten gates. Its massive wall is five and a half miles in circumference, and that of the fort is one and a half miles around, with two strongly fortified gates. Within this fort are the royal palace and mosque, and two fine audience halls. These buildings are all of beautiful marble, except the Diwan-i-Amm, or Hall of Audience for the Common People. That is a fine structure of red sandstone. The Diwan-i-Khass, or Hall of Select Audience, was the place where, more than anywhere else, Shah Jahan displayed his glory before the people. It is a fine open hall, with pillars and arches all of white marble. The pillars and cornices are beautifully ornamented with flowers in mosaic of precious stones and gilding, and on the latter at each corner of the hall, is sculptured and overlaid with gold the far-famed sentence, "If there be a Paradise on earth it is here."

The ceiling was once covered with silver filagree work, but it was taken off and coined by the Mahratta conquerors in 1759. It amounted to about eight hundred and fifty thousand dollars. The marble table on which stood the famous peacock throne is still there, but the golden peacocks no longer spread their jeweled tails beneath the pearl-fringed golden canopy under whose shelter the "king of the world" used to give audience to the nobles of his realm.

A parrot, cut out of a single emerald, stood between the two sparkling peacock tails; and two velvet umbrellas, fringed with pearls, stood on either side. These almost priceless gems of nature and art were all carried off by the Persian invader, Nadir Shah, in 1739.

The royal palace, baths, and mosque are all of marble, and, with the exception of the latter, are ornamented with mosaic of precious stones, arranged in flowers and fantastic designs, gilding and sculptured flowers in the cornices and around the windows of marble network. Much of this beautiful work has been defaced, and the stones extracted, and paint has been used to repair it.

The rooms for the women are small and low, but cool and bright—gilded cages they might well be termed; and, O! how weary the dark-eyed inmates must have become of their unvarying splendor! What longing glances they must have cast out of the marble lattice over the blue waters of the Jumna, and the hazy, far-reaching plains beyond!

It seems to have been the custom of the Moguls to name the royal mosque the *Pearl Mosque*, probably because they are built of such small but perfect proportions. The one here *is* a pearl—the pearl of mosques. It is a square platform of marble, with a wall on three sides, of the same material, with scalloped top, while on the fourth side is the place for prayer and preaching, surmounted by three pearl-like domes of dazzling whiteness and perfect symmetry. The stand where the preacher, or moulvai, stands, is ornamented with carved marble work of exquisite finish.

The past and present are placed in close juxtaposition within the walls of the Delhi fort. On one side are these beautiful and grand memorials of the past, and on the other stand several fine modern barracks for English soldiers; while the cabbages and onions of the soldiers' gardens flourish under the shadows of Shah Jahan's chaste and elegant creations.

There is a magnificent mosque outside the fort, and

not far from it, called the Jama Musjid, or "Clothes Mosque." There is always *one* such mosque at least in every Mahomedan city. The first word is often corrupted into *Jumma*, but the real word is Jama, or *clothes*, and is so named from the beautiful custom of having a store-room connected with the mosque, where clothing is kept for distribution to the needy among the faithful; and close by which, a saraee, or hotel, is always open for the reception of Mahomedan travelers, especially pilgrims to Mecca. They are fed and clothed gratis for a few days, and a small sum of money is given to each as he sets off again on his journey. Is not this custom worthy of being adopted and adapted by all Christian Churches?

The lovely Mumtaz Mahal never saw these beautiful palaces and mosques, for she had been moldering back to dust long before they were even conceived in the mind of Shah Jahan. But it is probable that she was the indirect cause of their erection, for the building of her surpassingly beautiful mausoleum brought so many skilled workman into the country, and was such a perfect success, that Shah Jahan's taste for fine architecture was developed, and he determined to build a new and more splendid Delhi.

Mumtaz Mahal, the favorite queen of Shah Jahan, the fifth Mogul emperor, was the daughter of Asof Khan, the brother of Noor Mahal, and was even more beautiful than her celebrated aunt. Her real name was Arzoomund Banoo Begum, and the title of Mumtaz Mahal, or the "Chosen of the Palace," was bestowed upon her by the king on account of his affection and preference for her above all the other inmates of the royal seraglio.

She was married to Shah Jahan in 1615, while he was only Prince Khurrum, and was greatly beloved and honored by him. She shared all his campaigns and perils, and rejoiced to see him surmount them all, but was not spared long to enjoy the pre-eminence so long waited and sought for. She died two years after he came to the throne. This event occurred during a campaign in the Deccan, on which she accompanied her husband.

When it became evident that she had only a few hours to live the king was sent for, and she made two requests of him. One was, that he should not exalt another wife to her position as queen; and the second was, that he would build a tomb for her that should command the admiration of the whole world.

He probably granted both these requests; certain it is that he fulfilled the latter. He long mourned his chosen and faithful companion, and the solace of the greater portion of his after life was to superintend the erection of the mausoleum, that should hand the name of his beloved queen, conjointly with his own, down to succeeding generations.

The remains of Mumtaz Mahal were carried to Agra and deposited in the beautiful garden where the mausoleum was afterward erected. It was her favorite resort when in the enjoyment of health and manifold earthly blessings. She passed many pleasant hours with her husband and children in its cool, fragrant groves, and it was probably selected by her as the spot where, " brief life and its fever o'er," the king and herself should be buried.

Shah Jahan, immediately upon his return to Agra, set about the work that lay upon his heart. He sent for various plans and models from different countries, and read descriptions of all the celebrated monuments he could hear of. At last an architect, who was sent to him by the sultan of Turkey, furnished him with the model of the Taj Mahal as it now stands.

The garden in which the Taj Mahal and the mosque, with its answering edifice, stand, lies on the bank of the Jumna river, about one mile east of the Agra fort. The road to it is cut through mounds of the ruins of ancient palaces. The entire garden is inclosed by a high wall of red sandstone, with cloisters around the interior. The lofty gateway is of the same material, surmounted by a row of small white marble domes. The whole structure is beautifully ornamented with white marble, in which are inscriptions from the Koran inlaid with black marble. The beautiful garden, which is kept in the finest order under the superintendence of an English gardener, is filled with every variety of flower, and shrub, and tree obtainable.

Lemon and orange, fig and mango, plantain, palm, bamboo, and cypress trees abound; while jasmine, honeysuckle, and various other flowering vines and plants perfume the air with their fragrant blossoms, and the bussorah, cloth of gold, and Marshal Neil roses vie with each other in sweetness.

The poinsetta, with its brilliant crimson leaves, and the eccentric cactus, and the angular, but fragrant-flowering gulaçheen, or China rose tree, with many other tropical growths, beautify this lovely spot, in the midst of which repose the ashes of Mumtaz Mahal and Shah Jahan in their right royal receptacle.

Several fountains are scattered throughout the premises, which, when at play, give a refreshing coolness to the atmosphere, and thus, in a measure, supply the only lacking charm of this exquisitely lovely spot.

The building stands upon a high platform of marble, with a lofty minaret at each corner. It is square, with the corners truncated or flattened, and is surmounted by a dome, the peculiarity of which is, that it is slightly smaller at its base than at its center. This unusual formation causes the illusion by moonlight of its seeming to expand, and the looker-on half expects to see it burst, and the whole fairy-like creation vanish like "the baseless fabric of a vision."

The dome is fifty feet in diameter by eighty in height. It tapers to a point, and is crowned by the significant crescent, that unfailing symbol of the Moslem. Four small domes cluster around the central and superior one. The four sides of the building are precisely alike. In the center of each is a high pointed arch, and these form the entrance to the apartment under the dome, in which are the tombs of the Mogul king and queen. Not the true ones; they are below on the ground floor, and are often decked with flowers by Mohamedan visitors; but these are directly above, and represent them.

Around these upper tombs is a marble screen six feet high, with one open space for entrance to them. The spaces on either side the pointed tops of the entrance arches, the tombs, and the narrow panels between the lattice-work slabs of the screen, are inlaid with precious stones in flowers. Jasper, lapis lazuli, agate, carnelian, bloodstone, onyx, amethyst, and other valuable and beautiful stones, were used in this work. The cornice and various parts of the room are inlaid with inscriptions from the Koran in black marble. Mahomedans claim that the whole of the Koran is thus inscribed upon the Taj, but that is, undoubtedly, an exaggeration. The room is wainscoted with the most delicately-sculptured flowers in bass-relief upon the marble panels.

The prevailing impression made upon the mind by this exquisite room is purity, the marble is so pure and so beautifully wrought and polished; while the gleams of color from the precious stones in the few places where they are used, serve to keep the apartment from seeming cold and gloomy.

There is a wonderful echo in the dome, which is delightful if only single notes are used, but it is painful to the ear otherwise.

The whole structure is of dazzling marble, almost entirely white, and is so perfect in all its details as to be without its equal in the world. It has been called a marble poem.

The following anonymous lines appeared in an English journal in India a few years ago :—

THE TAJ MAHAL.

"With minarets of marble rising stately from a sea
Of the dark-leaved mango's foliage streaked by the jaman tree,
Up to the empyrean where the crescent glitters bright,
Calm and unchanged still shining through the fall of Moslem might,
One majesty of whiteness the Taj of Agra stands,
Like no work of human builder, but a care of angel hands.
Look down the entrance vista through the lofty sandstone door;
How near it seems, though distant five hundred yards or more.
So down the shadowy vista of twice one hundred years
The past becomes the present, and the distant near appears,
And in a vision rises before the raptured eye
The splendor of the monarch who ruled in days gone by.
When 'neath the shade of snow-white domes, with pinnacles of gold,
In royal state, surrounded by pomp and wealth untold,
He sat dispensing justice, or discussed affairs of weight,
With councilors and princes of many a subject State;
Or when summoned to the conflict with a vast array he spurred,
To wreak upon Golconda the vengeance long deferred.
But see!—the sinking sun the fort in strong relief has brought,
Whose lengthening shadow forward creeps, as though it fondly thought
To reach the Taj and converse hold of glories passed away,
To hear the deeds of Shah Jahan and tell of Akbar's sway.

But the cruel sun in sinking turns the shadow from its goal,
And between, a bar forever, the Jumna's waters roll;
And as the light grows fainter, and clouds lose their golden rim,
The vision also changes, and its glory waxes dim.
The mighty realm is torn by strife, the notes of war resound;
Disgraced, deposed by filial hands, the monarch stands uncrowned!
His servants fled, for none were found of all the craven band
For the beleagured sovereign in peril firm to stand!
'Ere death call no man happy, lest the future evil bring,'
Such the moral history teaches to the peasant and the king.
But though the sovereign's sunset days were clouded o'er by ill,
A token of his glory—the Taj stands firmly still.
Majestic shrine of other days, to thee the power belongs
To resist the flight of ages and to awe the stranger-throng;
Long as the sacred Jumna o'er its bed of sand shall flow,
Thy glorious dome to heaven shall raise its massive breast of snow!
For the spirit of the monarch and the builder's art combine
To guard from lightning's levin-bolt, and time's decay, the shrine."

The common workmen on the Taj did not receive wages, but were daily supplied with food; but it is said that the officials, whose duty it was to deal out the rations, took such heavy toll that there was great distress and mortality among them. A poet of that time describing these events says the poor laborers used to cry out,

"O God, relieve our misery,
Else with the queen we also die!"

Twenty thousand workmen were seventeen years in building this mausoleum and the edifices connected with it.

The cost of the Taj was about nine million dollars. It is said that there were silver doors at the four arched entrances, and that they were taken away when the Jats conquered and sacked Agra.

The measurements of this celebrated spot are as follows:—

"The inclosure, including the garden and outer court, is a parallelogram of one thousand eight hundred and sixty feet by more than one thousand feet. The outer court (which is a saraee, or hotel) is surrounded by small rooms for travelers, built against the wall, and all opening into the central court-yard, and has four gateways. It is an oblong, occupying in length the whole breadth of the inclosure, and is about four hundred and fifty feet deep. The platform is eighteen feet high, and is an exact square of three hundred and thirteen feet each way. The four minarets at the corners are one hundred and thirty-three feet high, and are crowned with little open domes or pavilions. The mausoleum itself occupies a space of one hundred and eighty-six feet square in the center of the platform.

On the left of the Taj, from the garden side, is a mosque of red sandstone, with three marble domes; and on the right is a similar building, called the Juwab, or Answer, as it was built to preserve the symmetry of the whole design. This building is, in these latter days, often appropriated to the use of European travelers and parties of pleasure, and is thought to be a particularly suitable place for newly-married couples to reside during the honeymoon.

But we must now leave this wonderful creation, which can never be fully described by the pen of the writer nor portrayed by the brush of the artist, and follow the fortunes of its projector and builder.

After a series of campaigns in the Deccan, eight years in duration, peace was established, and the result to the Mogul Government was the acquisition of part of the kingdom of Ahmadnugger, and of an annual subsidy from the king of Golconda.

Meanwhile the Portuguese had obtained a foothold in Bengal. They had been allowed to establish a factory at Hooghly, and they had improved the opportunity afforded them by also building a fort and mounting it with guns. They soon grew insolent and rapacious, and their conduct was reported to the king. Shah Jahan had received a repulse from Michael Rodrigues, the head of the Portuguese colony, when he asked for assistance during his misfortunes, and he now sent the order, "Let the *idolaters* be immediately expelled from my dominions." Upon receiving this peremptory message, the Mogul viceroy in Bengal at once attacked the Portuguese and gained a complete victory over them. They killed over a thousand men, and took four thousand men and women prisoners. The most beautiful among the latter were forwarded to the king. This event occurred in 1632, and was the end of Portuguese power in Bengal.

In 1637 the Persian governor of Candahar rebelled

against his king, and made the province over to the Moguls, to whom it formerly belonged. He then sought refuge in the Mogul capital, where he was received with great favor by Shah Jahan, and was employed by him in military operations. Marshman says of this general, Ali Merdan, that "his fame has been perpetuated in India by the great public works which he executed, and more especially by the canal near Delhi, distinguished by his name, which has proved an incalculable blessing to the country it irrigates." It seems, therefore, that his talents were not confined to military tactics.

For the next ten years the Mogul Government carried on expensive and fruitless military operations beyond the river Indus, but at length relinquished their plans for conquest in that quarter. They were, however, obliged presently to take the field against the Persians, who had retaken Candahar. The Moguls made three efforts to recover their ancient inheritance, but were unsuccessful.

In 1655 Shah Jahan renewed offensive operations in the Deccan, and the war then begun continued for fifty years to harass the Mogul Government, and, doubtless, hastened its downfall. Aurungzebe, the third son of Shah Jahan, was the commander of the southern army, and conducted the war with mingled craft and bravery.

In 1656 the king of Golconda was defeated, and reduced to submission; and the succeeding year

Aurungzebe attacked the king of Beejapore, and would probably have extinguished the independence of that kingdom had not the news of his father's serious illness reached him just at the time. He was anxious to hasten to Agra, to join in the contest for the throne, and, having obtained a large sum of money from the king of Beejapore, he concluded a treaty whith him, and hastened, with his army, northward.

Shah Jahan had four sons, and each happened at this time to be in command of an army. Each was also of the opinion that he was well fitted to succeed his father, and *was willing, for the public good*, to take up the cares of Government. "Uneasy lies the head that wears a crown," and yet foolish mortals covet the glittering symbol of power even if accompanied with disquietude. In no event of life is the willingness to suffer for the good of others so brilliantly exemplified as when a responsible and honorable official position is in question.

Dara, the eldest son, was a talented and haughty man, and had been declared the successor to the throne by Shah Jahan. Soojah, the second son, was viceroy of Bengal, and was also a man of talent and energy, but was dissipated in his habits. Aurungzebe was able, ambitious, and cunning, and, unlike his brothers, who were free-thinkers, was a bigoted Mahomedan. Morad, the youngest, was a drunkard. Soojah, upon hearing the news, hastened from Bengal with his army.

Morad, the viceroy of Gunzerat, seized the public treasure of that province, and assumed the title of king. He then also, with his army, hastened toward the capital.

Aurungzebe, with his usual craftiness, determined to pretend to favor Morad, and joined him on the banks of the Nerbudda river. He saluted him as king, and assured him that it was the wish of his heart to see him firmly established on the throne, and when that should be happily accomplished he would renounce the world, and go on a pilgrimage to Mecca.

Dara had the advantage of being already at the capital, with the royal army and treasury at his command. He prepared to meet the two attacks by sending Raja Jai Sing to meet Soojah, and Raja Jesswunt Sing against the combined forces of Aurungzebe and Morad. It is an interesting fact that two Hindoo generals were sent in command of the imperial armies at so important a juncture, and it shows us that the policy of attaching the Hindoos to the Mogul Government by intermarriages, was at least partially successful. Just at this time Shah Jahan rallied, but it was too late to prevent fratricidal war.

Soojah was defeated near Benares, and retreated to Bengal; but in the conflict which ensued near the city of Ojain, between the forces of Aurungzebe and Morad and Jesswunt Sing, the latter was defeated, and the brothers advanced with thirty-five thousand troops toward Agra.

Dara came out to resist them with one hundred thousand foot, twenty thousand horse, and eight pieces of cannon. A terrific contest ensued, in which Dara was completely routed, and driven from the field with only two thousand men.

Aurungzebe then showed his true colors, and instead of advancing his brother's claims, as he had promised, quietly ignored them and placed himself at the head of the whole army. He at once took possession of the capital, deposed his father, and assumed control of the kingdom under the title of Alamgeer, that is, "Conqueror of the World."

Thus ended the thirty years' reign of Shah Jahan. He was sixty-seven years old when he was deposed by the ambitious and ungrateful Aurungzebe, and lived seven years longer, a prisoner in his own palace. He was treated with the greatest kindness and consideration by the king, but these last years would have been very lonely and sad for the aged monarch had he not been cheered and comforted by the presence and devotion of his lovely and devoted daughter, Jahanara Begum, who refused to join in the amusements of the Court, and gave herself entirely to the work of cheering the closing years of her father's life. This lady was a sister of Prince Dara, who was so ruthlessly supplanted by Aurungzebe. She was possessed of an amiable, loving disposition, and was of a religious turn of mind. Indeed "every virtue" adorned her character, if we may believe the flowery descriptions of Hindoostanee writers.

The tomb of this lady is to be seen by tourists, near several other exquisite mausoleums, in old Delhi, about five miles from the present city. It is not as fine a structure as one would naturally suppose would cover the remains of the favorite daughter of Shah Jahan. It is a simple tomb of white marble, with a cavity on the top filled with earth and sown to grass. The inscription, mostly written by herself, explains this unusual arrangement: "Let no rich canopy cover my grave. This grass is the fittest covering for the tomb of the poor in spirit; the humble, the short-lived Jahanara, the disciple of the holy men of *Chist*, the daughter of the king Shah Jahan." Her friends and admirers could not, however, allow her grave to be quite as unadorned as she wished. It is surrounded by a screen of marble network of the most exquisite design and finish.

There is a curious work of Jahanara Begum's in Delhi, which is interesting because it shows the admiration she had for her father's works. It is a miniature copy of the Jama Musjid, or Clothes Mosque, made of marble and delicately finished. But this choice memorial of the reign of Shah Jahan has been utilized by the English, by converting it into a commissariat bakery.

The glory of the Mogul dynasty culminated in

Shah Jahan's reign, and began to decline under Aurungzebe. During the latter's long reign of forty-nine years he pursued an entirely different policy from that of his forefathers. This change was probably caused by his being so stanch a Mahomedan. He did not favor the Hindoos, but, on the contrary, was so intolerant of their religious scruples that their hearts were turned from him; and even the Rajpoots, who had considered themselves identified with Mogul power, turned against him.

The wonderful rise of the Mahratta nation in the Deccan, and their determined hostility to the Moguls, formed another link in the chain of providential events by which God caused the Mogul dynasty, which appeared to be so strongly cemented, to slowly crumble to its fall.

Aurungzebe died in 1707, and the Mogul dynasty, although weakened and shattered, was not extinct when, nearly one hundred years later, the English army, under General Lake, gained a complete victory over a native army commanded by a French general at Delhi.

When the English took possession of the city they found a poor old blind man in the royal palace, who claimed to be the Mogul king. Lord Wellesley, the governor general of India at that time, desired to remove this shadow of a king to Monghyr, and so break the center of intrigue. But the royal family clung with such tenacity to their native city that the plan of their removal was not carried into execution; a great mistake, as was afterward manifest.

From this time forward Delhi was under the English Government, but a *pageant* of royalty was allowed to exist within the walls of the fort, and it became a hot-bed of treasonable plans and intrigues, which culminated in the Sepoy Rebellion of 1857.

Bahadur Shah, the puppet Mogul king, doubtless hoped to revive something of the former glory of the dynasty; but his ambition was the cause of his ruin, and by his perfidious treason against the power that had protected him from his enemies he only won for himself distress and exile. He died in Burmah, whither he and his family were transported after the suppression of the Rebellion, and his death closed the Mogul dynasty, which had existed in India for three centuries.

AHULIYA BAIE,

A Mahrattee Queen.

THE Mahrattas were originally of the Sudra caste, which is the fourth and lowest of the four great divisions of Hindoos, according to their sacred books; but, in spite of the numerous prohibitions against mingling with them, the Sudras have intermarried with the three higher castes very largely. The Mahrattas especially claim to have a large admixture of pure Brahmin blood in their composition, as well as of the two intermediate castes, and pride themselves accordingly. They occupy a tract of country on the western coast of India, south of the Nerbudda river. Their language is very similar to the Hindee. Their early history is involved in obscurity, but the modern city of Daulatabad has been identified as the site of a great commercial city of theirs, called Tagara, which was well known to the Romans more than two thousand years ago. They figure in history early in the sixteenth century, when the Mahomedans began to ravage the Deccan. They were the allies of Malik Ambar, a ruler of Abyssinian extraction, who for many years upheld the Ahmadnugger dynasty against the powerful Mogul kings Akbar and Jahangeer, and it was not till Shah Jahan bought over the principal Mahratta chiefs that he was defeated.

The defection of the Mahrattas at this time does not speak well for their sense of honor or their gratitude, as it was in the service of Malik Ambar that Shahjee, the father of the great Mahratta general, Sivajee, founded his fortunes.

The origin of this noted family is romantic. Mallojee, a Mahratta captain of horse, was employed by the king of Ahmadnugger about the close of the sixteenth century. His wife, who was childless, prayed for a son at the shrine of a Mahomedan saint, Shah Seffer by name. A son was afterward born to her, to whom she gave the name of Shahjee, in token of her gratitude to the saint. The name is a curious mingling of Persian and Hindee, Shah meaning "king," and jee being the Hindee term for "respect." Mallojee sought a wife for his son from a family of high standing, the head of which was called Jadoo Rao; but he refused to allow a daughter of his to marry into so plebeian a family. But soon after, in some fortunate raid, Mallojee obtained a large treasure, with which he bought some very large estates, including several cities, from the king of Ahmadnugger. Jadoo Rao became gracious at once, and the wedding ceremonies took place with great rejoicings and display. It is said that even the king of Ahmadnugger shed the light of his royal presence among the guests. Sivajee, the son of the couple so auspiciously married, was born in 1627, and was reared with great care by a Hindoo tutor of integrity and excellent abilities. But the lad, although expert in military knowledge and exercises, did not take kindly to book learning, and was never able to write or read.

After his father's death he gathered a small army and began a course of lawless marauding and plunder. In 1657, when Aurungzebe was campaigning in the Deccan, Sivajee professed himself a servant of the Mogul dynasty; but when Aurungzebe returned to Agra he began to plunder the Mogul territories in the Deccan, and even enlisted Mahomedans, whom Aurungzebe had dismissed, under his banner.

When Aurungzebe became king, Sivajee made his peace with him by affecting submission, but continued to loot indiscriminately, until a Mahomedan general, named Afzal Khan, was sent from Beejapore against him. Afzal Khan had great contempt for his adversary's prowess, and, when Sivajee proffered submission if he might only be pardoned, granted him an interview, when Sivajee was permitted to salute the Mahomedan officer, and took advantage of the opportunity thus afforded to assassinate him.

The Mahratta army then seized upon the Mahomedan troops and slaughtered them, and continued their predatory warfare up to the very gates of Beejapore. A fierce campaign ensued, and continued till Aurungzebe marched down into the Deccan with an immense army and compelled Sivajee to sue for peace. He was allowed to enter the Mogul service as a tributary, but managed to put an insidious claim in the agreement called "Chaut," the meaning of which is a fourth of the revenue, which was the occasion of great emolument to the Mahrattas, but of great trouble to the country.

Sivajee continued his intrigues and banditti warfare until 1674, when he seized upon a large territory and caused himself to be proclaimed king. He was weighed against gold and the money given to Brahmins, who were not at all pleased to find that he only weighed one hundred and forty pounds. After this his successes almost exceed belief, but they were cut short in 1680 by his death. His son, Sumbajee, reigned nine years, and was succeeded by his infant son, Sahoo. This lad was taken prisoner by the Moguls and retained by them seventeen years. They treated him with great kindness and allowed him to marry two wives, the daughters of some Mahratta nobles who were in the Mogul service. Perhaps they thought to tame the wild Mahratta instinct in the lad by kindness. Tara Baie, the widow of the regent who was to rule the Mahratta nation until Sahoo should return to his own, determined to retain the throne for her own son, and when the Moguls placed Sahoo in authority there ensued a division among the Mahrattas.

Sahoo was, however, the recognized king, but he was almost wholly indebted to his prime minister or "peshwa," Bajee Rao, for the success that followed his plans, for he had lost much of the national energy during his quiet life among the Moguls.

Bajee Rao managed every thing, and finally came in conflict with the general of the army, who thought he was taking the lion's share of the plunder. He marched to the city of Satara, where Bajee Rao was located, and attacked him; but a small force which the peshwa sent out against him overpowered him, and he was slain. Bajee Rao seemed to cherish no animosity, but bestowed the office upon the deceased general's son, an infant, and appointed a regent during his minority.

About this time the two great families of Holkar and Sindia were founded. Mulhar Rao Holkar was a herdsman, but entered the army and distinguished himself by such daring deeds that the peshwa, Bajee Rao, promoted him to the command of an expedition for levying contributions upon the province of Malwa. Sindia was allied to the Rajpoots, but was of the former caste. He entered the service of the peshwa, and was also promoted to posts of trust and emolument. Both of these men rose to great distinction as commanders in the Mahratta army.

Mulhar Rao Holkar, in some way not made plain in history, but probably as a reward for distinguished services, became ruler of several fine provinces, whose capital was Indore. His son and heir married Ahuliya Baie, a lady of the family of Sindia, but probably not of the one just mentioned. He died a few years after their marriage, leaving her with two children, a son named Mallee Rao, and a daughter named Mutcha Baie.

Upon the death of Mulhar Rao Holkar the succession devolved upon Mallee Rao, but he unfortunately soon developed symptoms of insanity, and died after nine months of suffering. According to Mahratta custom, Ahuliya Baie became at this juncture the only lawful ruler of the country, as her daughter had married into another family, and thereby lost her birthright.

The prime minister of the Holkar Government suggested that the widowed Ranee should adopt an heir, supposing, doubtless, that she would not be capable of governing her rude and rather turbulent people ; but she declined to act upon his suggestion, and assured him that she intended to occupy the position that, by right of Hindoo law and custom, was now hers. Her officers and army stood by her in this resolve, and the baffled minister tried to instigate outsiders against her. Madhoo Rao was the peshwa of the Mahratta Government at this time, and his uncle, the notorious Ragoba, held a command in the army. The Holkar minister offered this chief a large bribe if he would come with his army and assist him to dethrone Ahuliya Baie. He consented, and began to make preparations for the campaign ; but the courageous Ranee hearing of his design, began to make such vigorous preparations for war that he began to waver in his determination. She sent him a message, to the effect that he would only disgrace himself by making war upon a woman, and trying to deprive her of her rights, and advised him to desist. She avowed her firm resolve to lead her army in person, and caused the howdah for her elephant to be fitted up with bows and arrows. These demonstrations were not without effect. Ragoba sought further aid from the Mahratta chiefs, but Sindia and others refused to aid him in making war upon a brave and high-minded woman, and the peshwa at length ordered his uncle to refrain from intermeddling in the affairs of the Holkar family. This settled the matter at once, and Ahuliya Baie, then about thirty years of age, entered upon her duties as the ruler of the Holkar possessions.

The position was an honorable and highly responsible one, and she seems to have so understood it. She was a firm believer in the Hindoo religion, and at this important juncture she consulted with the priests upon all matters pertaining to the State, believing them to be the only safe guides in both temporal and spiritual things.

A large amount of money was in the treasury when she came into possession, and her first act of sovereignty was to consecrate this treasure to religious charities. The ceremony consisted in putting a few leaves of the sacred toolsee plant in water, which was afterward sprinkled over the royal treasury, a Brahmin meanwhile uttering the words of consecration. She then began to consider the best plan of perpetuating the dynasty. She was prevented from marrying again by Hindoo law, and her daughter was severed from the succession. At length she selected Tokajee Holkar, an officer of good repute, although not a member of her husband's family, to act as commander-in-chief of the army, probably intending him to succeed her in the Government. Her keen discrimination of character was not at fault in this choice.

Tokajee Holkar became her most faithful and wise viceroy in the distant territories of her possessions, and never gave her reason to repent her choice. According to eastern usage, he always spoke of the Ranee Ahuliya Baie as his mother, and she always spoke of him as the son of Mulhar Rao Hulkar, thus openly avowing his heirship to the succession. With great magnanimity she forgave the prime minister his opposition to her cause, and upon receiving assurances of his fidelity in the future re-instated him in his office, and, so far as we can judge, he was "faithful to his salt" ever afterward.

The managers of the different posts in and around Indore were mostly Brahmins, and it appears from history that they must have discharged their duties with singular fidelity. The policy of Ahuliya Baie was that of kindness and conciliation. Although so strict a devotee of the Hindoo religion, she was interested in the welfare of all her subjects, even in the wild hill tribes of Goands and Bheels, who were simply robbers and marauders.

By wise and conciliatory, though strict, measures she succeeded in bringing them into a much higher state of civilization. But it was among the Mahratta people proper that the enlightened policy of this Hindoo queen produced the most excellent results. Instead of enormous taxes to support an expensive administration, as is generally the case among Hindoostanee rulers, she strove, by moderate assessment and wise protective legislation, to encourage her people in the peaceful arts. It is usual for native rulers to watch narrowly, through their agents, the success of merchants and craftsmen, and, if they have any extra good fortune, to demand at once a large proportion of their gains for the royal treasury. It was formerly the custom, and still is in the principalities under native rule, for men who are in reality merchant princes to dress shabbily and to carefully conceal their true income; but in the dominions of Ahuliya Baic men could rise to affluence by honest labor or trade, and be assured that their queen was well pleased to see their prosperity, and would protect them and their possessions. All turbulent and mischievous persons were dealt with in a way to keep that class in awe, and to re-assure the law abiding portion of the population. Indeed, so marked is the difference between the historical account of the reign of Ahuliya Baie and those of contemporary Hindoo princes, that it is like suddenly arriving, through rough seas and driving storms, in a lovely, quiet haven in some peaceful island.

During her reign of thirty years' duration the internal peace of the country was not once broken, and only once was there trouble from without. The Rana of Oodipore once invaded her territories, but she brought such a well-disciplined army against him that he was soon obliged to retrace his steps. Her exemption from foreign invasion seems almost miraculous, for in those days kings seemed to be always "going forth to battle."

Probably the great reason why her administration was so uniformly successful in dealing with all classes of people so satisfactorily, was that she avoided change of State officers as much as possible. She therefore maintained a uniform method of carrying out her measures. This is particularly pleasing to the native mind. They dislike extremely any change of land tenure and revenue laws, or in the methods used to enforce them, as they expect they will in some way work to their disadvantage.

There is something wonderfully beautiful in the character of this heathen queen. Living as she did among a people wholly devoid of the light of Christianity, and entirely ignorant as she was of both the law and the Gospel; she seems to have embodied in her daily life their principles, doing "by nature the things contained in the law."

The historian says of her that she "used to rise early, about an hour before daybreak, to say her prayers and perform the customary ceremonies. She then heard the sacred volumes of her faith read for a fixed period, distributed alms, and gave food in person to a number of Brahmins. Her own food was then brought, which consisted simply of vegetables; for, although meat was not prohibited to her tribe, she had foresworn all animal food. Retiring after breakfast for a little repose, she would rise about two o'clock, dress herself, and proceed to the durbar, or court, where she remained till six in the evening hearing complaints in person. Two or three hours were then taken for refreshment and worship, when she again held court for two hours, retiring to rest about eleven o'clock."

Not a life of ease and luxury was this, but a conscientious performance of the duties of her position. She is said to have declared that she knew she must answer to God for every exercise of power. Happy would it be for the nations of the earth did all rulers remember this great fact and act accordingly!

Several forts and public works were constructed during her reign, one of the most noted of which was a road over the Vindhya Mountains, a herculean undertaking accomplished at great expense. But the greatest work of her reign was the building of the present city of Indore. The old city was merely a large, irregular village, but the new one, although not pretentious, was worthy of its name.

Although relying greatly upon the counsels of the Brahmins, Ahuliya Baie retained her independence of judgment and supremacy in State politics. There were envoys from most of the other Indian courts at Indore, who all agreed in ascribing the utmost independence of action to her. Still it is evident that the Brahmins enjoyed a golden age during her reign. They were her deputies in all the chief cities of India, and were the almoners of her bounty to the poor and diseased, to pilgrims and travelers. Wells and rest-houses were built on the main lines of travel throughout her territories, and at Jagahnath, Gya, Benares, Kedarnath, and other places, she erected houses for pilgrims and priests, and sent sums annually for their maintenance. The temple of Biseswara, at Benares, and of Mahadeo, at Gya, were built by her.

Ahuliya Baie was not beautiful in person, although of agreeable presence and pleasing demeanor. She was of medium height and slight figure, and her complexion was rather dark. It is said that the wife of Ragoba once sent a female attendant to the Court of Ahuliya Baie as a sort of spy, merely to gratify her curiosity as to the personal appearance of so celebrated a woman. The report brought was, "that the Ranee has not beautiful features, but a heavenly light is on her countenance."

But she was endowed with what is of far greater value than beauty, fine perceptive faculties, good sense, and a high moral nature. She could read, and was well versed in the *Puranas.* These sacred books are of much later compilation than the Vedas, the oldest being about one thousand years old, and the latest about four hundred and fifty.

She paid strict regard to Hindoo usage in the matter of dress, as in all else, and never wore the rich attire of royalty; but dressed, according to the rules laid down for widows, in pure white, and discarded all jewelry except a small gold necklace. In the daily routine of her onerous duties, only broken by the stated religious festivals of her faith, the life of Ahuliya Baie glided along.

Her people learned to trust and love her as their benefactress, and both high and low would have esteemed it a sacrilege to do her wrong. The neighboring princes, too, viewed her course with admiration, and treated her with the same respect they did the peshwa of the Mahratta nation.

She was strangely free from vanity, which is usually supposed to be inseparable from the feminine character. One of the Brahmins wrote a book in her praise, in which her virtues were extolled to the skies, and presented it to her. She heard it read, and remarked when it was finished, "I am a weak, sinful woman, and undeserving of such fine encomiums." She then ordered it to be thrown into the river close by, and took no notice of the author. But the unhallowed teachings of the Hindoo religion brought deep affliction upon this interesting queen at last. Her daughter's husband died, and the daughter, Mutchta Baie, declared her intention of being burned with his body.

Ahuliya Baie, now an aged woman, entreated her daughter not to leave her without kin upon the earth, but to live for her sake. The poor misguided woman was, however, resolved to perform the dreadful rite, in the vain hope of winning eternal happiness by this one great, meritorious act. In reply to her mother's entreaties, she said: "You are aged, my mother, and a few years will end your pious life; my only child and husband are gone, and when you follow, life will be insupportable to me, but the opportunity of ending it with honor will then have passed."

The unhappy Ranee could not dissuade her daughter from her resolution, and at last desisted from the attempt, and reluctantly consented that her wish should be carried out. She even so far prevailed over the natural anguish and dread a mother could but feel at such a time as to join in the procession, and be present near the funeral pyre during the dreadful ceremony.

Two Brahmins supported her, and endeavored to keep up her semblance of calmness and resignation. The widow mounted the fatal pile, and, having distributed her clothing and jewels to her nearest relatives, according to the custom of the Deccan, sat down on the pile, and took the head of her deceased husband in her lap. With her own hand she then applied a torch to the pile, and the dry wood crackled, and great tongues of flame darted up all around her. The priests and the multitude began to shout and howl, that her shrieks of agony might not be heard. The self-possession of the poor mother gave way at the fearful sight, and, with loud cries, she tried to rush forward and snatch her daughter from the blazing pile; but her two attendant Brahmins quickly seized her arms, and detained her in her place. The pile, with its human freight, was soon reduced to a small heap of ashes, and the deed of self-immolation was consummated.

The afflicted mother, with the calmness of despair, bathed, with the other spectators, in the river near which the unholy deed was perpetrated, and then withdrew to the royal palace, probably the most sorrowful woman in all her dominions. She remained for several days bowed with grief, and unable to converse, but she then rallied, and tried to console herself in building a monument to the memory of her daughter.

It must sadden the hearts of our readers to contemplate this noble, sincere woman, with her heart full of benevolent intent, and her hands of kindly deeds, going down into the valley of the shadow of death with no Divine radiance to cheer her way.

Poor Ahuliya Baie! Although the queen of a million of people, she was poorer than the humblest Christian woman of to-day who can sing in the assurance of faith,

> " I shall find down the valley no alarms,
> For my Saviour's blessed smile I can see;
> He will bear me in his loving, mighty arms;
> There's a light in the valley for me."

And yet she may stand far higher in the great day to which creation hastens, than many foolish ones in Christian lands who refuse to accept the proffered love of God through Christ Jesus.

Ahuliya Baie died in 1795, at the age of sixty, leaving a name for piety and wise legislation which any ruler might envy, and to this day any usage or point of law that can be upheld by reference to her practice is unquestionably right in the estimation of native courts. She was long mourned by her subjects, and her reign is always spoken of in that region as the "flourishing period."

The Brahmins placed a statue of Ahuliya Baie by the stone figures of Rama and Seeta, his wife, and she, too, is considered one of the "avatars," or incarnations of the deity.

Tokajee Holkar succeeded her, but died two years later. His sons quarreled, and fought for the preeminence; and a predatory warfare was kept up for twenty years, when the State submitted to British authority.

KISHNA COMAREE BAIE;

Or, the Maiden's Sacrifice.

THE heroine whose short, tragical life is sketched in these pages was princess of the house of Oodipore, the most noble of the princes of that section of India called Rajpootana.

The chief reason assigned for this pre-eminence is that the Oodipore family trace their descent to *Loh*, the eldest son of Rama, the great hero who flourished about twelve hundred years before Christ.

There is no doubt that such a prince existed at some period in the past, but tradition and history are so intermingled in Hindoo annals that it is sometimes difficult to separate them.

Rama was married to Seeta, who, like himself, belonged to the Solar race of Hindoos in the province of *Oude;* hence the name of the family.

It is supposed that the early Hindoos were divided into two great bodies called the Solar and Lunar races, and many wild and fanciful legends in regard to the warfare carried on between them are related in the poetical histories of the people. The wife of Rama was carried off by Ravana, the king of Ceylon, and Rama having formed an alliance with Hanooman, the king of the monkey tribe, set out on an expedition to Ceylon to recover his bride. But when they reached the southern boundary of India, the Straits of Manaar lay between them and Ceylon, and they were not provided with boats, nor could they obtain them. Here the monkeys rendered most valuable assistance. They flew back over the broad, dusty plains of Hindoostan to the gigantic Himalaya Mountains, the lofty "abode of snow," that separates between India and northern Asia, and quickly loaded themselves with great stones and returned to the expectant army. A bridge was constructed of the stones in a short time, and the working committee, seeing the bridge was nearly completed, sent a deputation to meet a supply party of monkeys and tell them to drop their burdens just where they were and hasten on to the conflict. They obeyed with alacrity, and the stones they dropped formed the Vindhya range of mountains, that stretches nearly across Central India. The ledge of rocks across the straits, called Adam's Bridge, is supposed by Hindoos to be the bridge built by Rama.

The beautiful Seeta was rescued, and the army returned triumphant. Soon after, Rama accidentally killed his brother and cast him into a river, and was, they believe, reunited to the Deity. He is called an *avatar*, or "Incarnation of God," and is worshiped by multitudes of people. Many of the festivals celebrated by Hindoos are in commemoration of the exploits of Rama.

The descendants of Prince Loh, the eldest son of Rama, migrated to Surat, and occupied that country for a long time. Their capital was the city of Balabipore, on the Gulf of Cambay. About A. D. 524 the king of Persia sent an army against them, and the capital was taken and sacked. The wife of the reigning Raja, with a few adherents, fled to a cave, where, soon afterward, a son was born to her whom she named "*Goha*," that is, "Cave," on account of the circumstances of his birth. The remnants of the scattered tribe gradually rallied around this last scion of their house and established themselves at Edur. They must have flourished greatly, and been admitted to the friendship of the Persians; for we learn that Goha, the cave-born Raja, married the granddaughter of the Persian king, whose wife was the daughter of Maurice, the Christian emperor of Constantinople. Goha was the founder of the modern Oodipore family, and an historian remarks in regard to its origin: "We are led to the singular conclusion that the Hindoo *sooraj*, or *sun*, the descendant of a hundred kings, the undisputed possessor of the honors of Rama, the patriarch of the Solar race, from whom other Hindoo princes, before they succeed to the throne of their fathers, must obtain the "talook," or sign of royalty and investiture, is, in fact, the offspring of a Christian princess."

There were nine rulers of the Goha line who reigned successively in Edur, but the ninth was murdered by his own sons while hunting. The Ranee, with her infant son, was hurried off to a distant part of the country, where she dwelt among shepherds until her son Bappa grew to manhood. She then revealed to him his royal parentage, and the ambition of the lad was stirred at once. He sent messengers as far as possible to collect the scattered followers of his house, and having gathered a small band, proceeded with them to the city of Chitore, and presented himself and his claims to the reigning Raja. He was well received by the Raja, but the nobles of the court were angry that an unknown youth should receive so much attention. Just then Chitore was invaded by a foreign foe, and no general could be found who was willing to lead on the army against the invaders. Bappa tendered his services to the Raja and they were accepted. He advanced, at the head of the State army, against their foes, and completely defeated them. On the return of the victorious army, Bappa was received with acclamation by all the people and was placed on the throne of Chitore. From him are descended the long line of princes who have in succession borne the title of Rana of Oodipore.

Many centuries passed away before the date of our story. The descendants of Bappa became a numerous people and built a large city, which they named Oodipore, in commemoration of their fatherland, the famous province of Ayodh, the modern Oude.

About the beginning of the present century the East India Company, then in control of British power in India, withdrew their protection from the territories west of the Jumna river, where they had previously interfered somewhat to prevent unlimited anarchy.

The Mahrattas and Mahomedans were thus left unchecked to prey upon the rich and populous Rajpootana States.

The Rana of Oodipore had at this time a beautiful daughter, about sixteen years of age. She was named Kishna Comaree. The last name is that of a goddess, said to be one of the incarnations of Parbuttee, the wife of Shiva, the third person of the Hindoo Triad. Cape Comorin, the southern extremity of Hindoostan, is named from this incarnation. She was very beautiful, in mind as well as person, and was styled the "Flower of Rajpootana."

There was considerable rivalry among the neighboring Rajas as to who should be honored with her hand. Aside from the loveliness of the fair Kishna, it was considered a great honor to be allied to the ancient house of Oodipore, and there were jealous heart-burnings among the aspirants, until at last the question was settled by the formal announcement that Raja Bheem Sing, of Jodhpore, and the Princess Kishna Comaree were betrothed. But shortly afterward the Raja died, and the question was again an open one. It seems from this that the betrothal ceremonies had not taken place, and Kishna was not considered a widow.

Juggut Sing, the Raja of Jeypore, immediately sent proposals of marriage to her, and was accepted. He sent a band of soldiers to escort her to his capital, but they never reached Oodipore, as Raja Man Sing, the successor of Bheem Sing upon the throne of Jodhpore, put in a claim for the princess' hand, on the plea that the marriage was contracted with the *throne* rather than its occupant. He attacked and routed the men sent by the Raja of Jeypore, and thereby drew the whole country into turmoil and war. The Raja of Jeypore brought a large army into the field to sustain his claim, and was joined by Ameer Khan, a Mahomedan freebooter, and two Mahratta generals from the army of the powerful chief, Sindia. A Jodhpore noble, who hated Raja Man Sing, also joined him, and with his army greatly strengthened by these allies he engaged the Jodhpore forces in action. A fiercely contested battle ensued in which the Raja of Jeypore was victorious. This occurred in February, 1807.

Raja Man Sing retreated to Jodhpore, and shut himself up in the fort with those of his officers and men who survived and remained faithful. He was besieged for several months while his country was laid waste by his foes. In this extremity he attempted to buy over to his cause the Mahomedan robber, Ameer Khan, who, on the promise of fifty-four lacs of rupees, or two million seven hundred thousand dollars, changed sides, and began to plunder the dominions of the Raja of Jeypore.

Man Sing was considerably elated at this turn of fortune, and resolved to see if his star would not continue in the ascendant. He wished the Jodhpore noble, Shiva Sing, who had turned against him, put out of the way, and the wicked Ameer Khan readily agreed to do this also for an additional sum of five hundred thousand dollars. In order to carry out this design he pretended to desert Raja Man Sing's cause, and afterward paid Shiva Sing a visit in his native city of Tagore. The noble was wary, and did not at first give credence to the Mahomedan's story; but when he took his oath on the Koran that he was sincere in his statement, Shiva Sing could no longer doubt.

Shortly after, Ameer Khan invited Shiva Sing and his followers to an entertainment in a large tent, and when they were absorbed in watching the mazy evolutions of some dancing girls, he caused the ropes of the tent to be cut, and it fell upon them, catching them as in a net. He then ordered his men to fire upon them, and they were all slaughtered.

Kishna, the innocent cause of all this bloodshed, was, doubtless, very unhappy at the wide-spread devastation and loss of life occasioned by the feud between the two rivals, especially as the provinces of her father were also subjected to plunder by the armies of Ameer Khan and Sindia. There were the large armies, and they must be fed; and although the Rana of Oodipore had not joined in the conflict, he could not save his flourishing lands from being overrun. Prosperous villages and fruitful fields were daily turned into desert places, and the distress of the people was extreme. The Rana was overwhelmed with sorrow, and sent to beg the British Government to protect his territories, offering to cede half of them to the English if they would protect the other half.

But the obstinacy and cruel indifference of the Government at that time seems unaccountable. They persisted in the newly-promulgated policy of non-interference, and the Rana, in despair, made an agreement with Ameer Khan, in which he made over one fourth of his dominions to him with the understanding that he should let the remainder alone. He even submitted to the ignominy of exchanging turbans with the robber chief, an eastern mode of expressing equality and alliance between rulers.

Now we come to the last act of this fearful drama. The infamous Ameer Khan and a vile Hindoo favorite of the Rana, named Ajeet Sing, suggested to him that he could easily put an end to the wars that were ruining the whole country of Rajpootana by putting the young Kishna to death, and thus removing the cause of the enmity between the chieftains. Ameer Khan declared if this was not done he would seize the princess and carry her by force to Raja Man Sing.

Overcome by the difficulties of his position, and overborne by his persistent and blood-thirsty advisers, the Rana at length consented to sacrifice his daughter. But here a new difficulty arose. Who would perform the deed? Raja Daulat Sing, a distant kinsman, was asked to take her life, but he indignantly replied,

"Accursed be the tongue that commands it; dust be on my allegiance if it must be preserved in this manner!"

At length a brother of the Rana agreed to perform the atrocious deed. He waited, tulwar in hand, for the appearance of Kishna, whom he had summoned to his presence; but her innocent loveliness so touched his heart that he, too, refused to take her life. By this time the whole family became aware of the dreadful purpose had in view, and it seems wonderful that so recently as the beginning of this century no alternative could be thought of by any member of the family. The false and detestable notions of family and caste *honor* must be upheld, even by the perpetration of murder!

The poor mother of the princess became frantic with grief and rage when the fell design became apparent to her, and called upon the gods to curse the instigator of the scheme; but Kishna, who seems to have fully comprehended the futility of resistance, sought to console her mother by appealing to her courage and the stoical principles of their religion.

"Why afflict yourself, my mother," she said, "at this shortening of the sorrows of life? I fear not to die, am I not your daughter? Why, then, should I fear death? We are marked out for sacrifice from our birth, and only enter the world but to be sent out of it again. Let me thank my father that I have lived so long."

At last a sister of the Rana, named Chand Baie, prepared a bowl of poison composed of flowers and herbs with a deadly opiate. She presented this to Kishna and adjured her to drink it for the sake of her father's honor and the welfare of her country. Kishna bowed and said, "This is the marriage to which I was fated," and drank a portion of the mixture. This proving ineffectual, she drank the second and the third time of the poisonous draught, when, with a prayer for blessings upon her father, she fell asleep and never woke again. The unhappy mother only survived the loss of her beloved daughter a few days, when her remains followed the body of Kishna to the funeral pyre.

When news of this dastardly deed reached the public the indignation and grief of the nobles and people knew no bounds, and the Rana and his advisers were overwhelmed with their reproaches and execrations. One of the chiefs of the family, to whom word was sent of the deed in contemplation, rode in hot haste to the Court in order to protest against it, and finding himself too late, unfastened his sword and shield, and placed them at the feet of the Rana with the words: "My ancestors have served yours for thirty generations, but never more shall these arms be used in your service."

The sacrifice of the innocent and lovely princess brought, of course, no real advantage to the house of Oodipore. Its territories continued to suffer from plunder, and the people could not continue the cultivation of the lands, nor carry on their trades to advantage. The consequence was that the revenue decreased rapidly, until it only amounted to about one hundred thousand dollars per annum.

In 1817 the British Government in India resolved to give up the neutral policy, and notified the native States of their determination, and proposed to them a general alliance for their protection and improvement. The Rajas and chiefs hailed this offer with joy and embraced it readily. The Raja of Jodhpore gladly joined the alliance, and the proud Rana of Oodipore began to consider the subject, as well he might in the despoiled and demoralized condition of his kingdom.

It was the boast of the Oodipore rulers that they had never acknowledged the sovereignty of the Moguls or Mahrattas, nor contaminated their blood by intermarriages with either people; but the protection and rule of the white-faced foreigners who, as the Rana remarked, "had come in ships from a country *before unknown*," was quite another thing, and he thankfully accepted it. The last Rajpoot chief who came into the alliance was the Raja of Jeypore; but he at length, seeing there was no help for it, made a virtue of necessity and joined in the compact. The debasing superstitions of the Hindoo religion are no longer allowed to crush out the natural affection of human hearts by prompting to cruel and unholy deeds; but while we rejoice in this fact, we deeply regret that this state of things was not inaugurated in time to save the life of the lovely princess of Oodipore, which was sacrificed by craven and cruel men in the fallacious hope of thereby gaining peace and safety without danger to themselves.

KISHNA'S FAREWELL.

"My father, willingly for thee
  And for my native land I die;
At thy behest my life was spared,*
  I give it now without a sigh.
This is my *fated*† marriage, writ
  By mystic fingers on my brow
When I a tender infant lay;
  The doom is consummated now.
And, father, if my early death
  But quell the storm of bloody strife,
Surely the gods will smile on me
  Who, to bring peace, lay down my life.
And then, perchance, in some fair form
  Of singing bird, or flowering tree,‡

* The Rajpoots suffered but few of their daughters to live.

† Hindoos believe that a certain god writes the fate of every child on its forehead the sixth day after its birth.

‡ Hindoos believe in the transmigration of souls, and ultimate absorption into the Deity. Their ideas of the future state are very vague.

They'll suffer me on earth to dwell,
  And song or shelter yield to thee.
And if a bul-bul's * mellow note
  Should cheer thee in some vigil-hour,
And thrill thy heart with tenderness
  And nerve thee with mysterious power;
Or if, when 'neath the mango's shade
  Thou seek'st relief from noonday glare,
A grateful coolness round thee steal
  And subtle fragrance fill the air;
Then know 'tis Kishna hovering near
  To comfort and to strengthen thee,
Permitted in the after life
A minister of good to be.

* * * * * *

Nay, nay, my mother, why these tears?
  This is to thee no stranger-pain;
My infant sisters only drew
  Their breath to yield it up again.
I thank my father for the years
  Passed in this world, so wondrous fair,
In the bright sunshine of thy love,
  And circled with thy guardian care.
I am *thy* daughter, therefore brave,
  I fear not death nor funeral fire;
They but assist my longing soul
  To reach the goal of its desire.
Farewell, farewell! my eyelids close;
  Strange power my heart-throbs seems to quell.
The favor of the gods be yours,
  My father—mother—all, farewell.

* Bul-bul, the nightingale.

THE RANEE OF JHANSEE,

A Tale of the Indian Mutiny.

THE province of Jhansee was tributary to the Mahratta Government when it first came to the particular notice of the English.

In 1804 a treaty was concluded with "the man in possession," Sheo Rao Bhao, who was a sort of governor with limited powers, and in 1817 the peshwa of the Mahrattas ceded his rights in the territory to the East India Company.

The governor general of India was pleased at this time to make the province of Jhansee hereditary in the family of Sheo Rao Bhao, who had died a short time previously, leaving his rights to his grandson, Rao Ramchunder.

In 1832 the governor general bestowed the title of Raja on Rao Ramchunder, and concluded a treaty with him; but the newly-made noble only enjoyed his honors three years, when he also died. He left no son, but adopted one just before his death. This was according to the custom in native principalities; but Sir Charles Metcalfe, governor of Agra, who had the supervision of Jhansee, decided that this usage ought not to prevail in a dynasty created by the English. He, therefore, caused a son of Sheo Rao

Bhao, a leper, to assume the rule. He died in 1838, and was succeeded by his brother, the only remaining son of Sheo Rao. This man, Raja Gungadhur, died in 1853, and, in spite of the former decision of the governor, adopted a son just before his death. The Ranee of Jhansee was a woman of superior mental endowments and high physical courage, and she determined to prosecute the lad's claim.

Lord Dalhousie, then governor general of India, after mature deliberation, decided, as in the former case, in regard to the adoption of an heir, that as there was no lawful claimant to the throne, the dynasty should lapse, and that the province should come under direct English rule.

This decision was a death-blow to the ambitious aspirations of the Ranee, who had hoped, as regent during the minority of the adopted heir, to taste the sweets of power and wealth.

No doubt she cursed the arrogant *Feringhees*, as they style the English, in her heart, and longed for an opportunity of taking revenge. That opportunity soon came, and the fiery but smoldering passions that had been pent up in her breast burst forth like Vesuvius in action !

The hot season of 1857 opened its fierce fires and sirocco blasts over the plains of Hindoostan, and more pitiless than the elements was the storm of revengeful fury that broke over the heads of the English residents, scattered in handfuls here and there throughout the land, at the mercy of their suddenly uprising foes.

Why *every* foreigner, man, woman, and child, was not cut off has puzzled many to understand. Doubtless the reason, aside from the great fact of an overruling Providence, was that the great body of the people felt kindly toward the English Government. It had rescued many provinces from devastating invasions, and the misrule of unprincipled and dissolute princes. It had assumed the control of several provinces *at the request of the people,* thus showing, beyond a doubt, that the careful administration of justice which always prevailed in the dominions under English control was appreciated by the orderly and industrious part of the population. But, for the same reason, English rule was a terror to evil doers, both among princes and people, and these disaffected villains, both Hindoo and Mahomedan, although bitterly hating each other, joined in league against the English.

The memory of the successive outbreaks and scenes of brutal slaughter is still fresh in our minds, as is also that of the quick retribution, and the re-establishment of British power in India.

The shortsightedness of the disaffected nobles and soldiery in supposing it possible that they could *retain* possession of the country for any considerable time, can only be accounted for by the blinding influence of a spirit of revenge and hate. There was but little to hinder their cutting off the few English residents and regiments in the land, but then all England would have risen to repossess the country. Some native rulers were wise enough to comprehend the true state of the case, and when importuned to join the rebels refused to do so. Jung Bahadoor, the prime minister and real ruler of Nepal in the Himalayas, was urged again and again to assist the mutineers, and gave an unqualified refusal. When pressed for his reasons, he answered, "I have seen *Woolwich*, and know how this matter will end." He had visited England, and seen the Military Academy and stores at Woolwich, and understood somewhat the immense resources of the English nation.

Many were true to the English at great risk to themselves. A wealthy Hindoo banker in Bareilly, who had long professed great friendship for the English, took charge of some valuable plate belonging to the ruling officer of the province when he with every other white-face had to flee to the mountains. The city was soon in the hands of the insurgents, and Khan Bahadoor Khan assumed command of the place.

The banker's former relations with the English were well known, and it was believed that he had valuable property of theirs in his keeping, so he was shortly visited and the treasure demanded. He remained entirely reticent on the subject, and they could make nothing of him. They abused and threatened, and finally tied him across the mouth of a cannon, and would undoubtedly have blown him away from it, had not a conflict between the Hindoos and Mahomedans just then broken out in the city, which compelled their attention elsewhere. A pacific policy toward Hindoos was pursued after this, and he was left unmolested. Word reached him afterward that some English refugees from a neighboring city were hiding in some villages in the district, and, bringing native cunning to his aid, he contrived to send money to them, by which means they were able to secure their safety. This man was generously rewarded a few months afterward by the gift of several fine estates and the title of Raja—both to be hereditary in his family.

The faithfulness of the Mahomedan ruler of Rampore was even more remarkable than the case we have mentioned, as the Mahomedans were the *inciters* of the whole movement of rebellion, and fully intended to be the chief profiters by it. Their *religious* enthusiasm, too, was far greater than that of the Hindoos, as the latter only wished to be let alone, and not have their religious superstitions infringed upon, while the Mahomedans longed to win back India for God and his prophet.

Rampore was surrounded by a country wholly under the sway of the mutineers, except on the north, where the Himalayas tower in calm, majestic grandeur, and in whose green recesses at Nynee Tal and Almora had gathered the fugitive families of English residents from Bareilly, Moradabad, and Budaon. They were protected by Goorka soldiers, whose faithfulness had been secured by the promise of a large reward from the commissioner of Kumaon and Gurhwal, a gentleman in whose word natives had the most perfect confidence.

Rampore was full of a turbulent and semi-civilized people who were eager to join in the conflict. But the Nuwab succeeded in restraining them and in maintaining his own views and plan of action, though often at great risk to himself. Supplies were sent continually to the fugitives in Nynee Tal, greatly to their comfort. More than this he could not do with safety.

The Nuwab, too, learned shortly that ingratitude is not a trait of the English character.

The faithfulness of domestic servants during that fearful time was very remarkable. If they had simply "struck work," and run away from the families and regiments they served, the whole British nation might have taken up arms in vain. The terrible Indian *sun* is an enemy that valor cannot subdue. It was—humanly speaking—the faithfulness of the domestic servants of India that enabled the English army to win back that country to the British Government.

Many other nobles, besides those we have mentioned, were wise in looking forward, instead of being misled by the appearances of the present, but the Ranee of Jhansee was not one of them. Had she but showed kindness to the English refugees, and thrown the weight of her influence in favor of loyalty to the English, she would have, without doubt, secured the wish of her heart; but, embittered and maddened by the fancied ill-treatment she had received from the English Government, she hailed with joy the prospect of being able to regain her power and wreak her revenge. She sent her emissaries among the native soldiery stationed in Jhansee, exhorting them to be in readiness for rising when the signal should be given. The English officers well knew that the crisis would soon come, but there was no alternative, they must remain and meet it.

On the first of June it became evident that the storm was about to burst, and all the English residents were ordered to take refuge in the fort. Upon the fourth day of June the soldiers took the offensive and besieged the little handful of English, who were, of course, unable to hold out long against such superior numbers. They offered to surrender if they might leave the place. This was granted them, and they marched out of the fort, hoping to get out of the city in safety, and take the chance of escape in the country round about.

But the Ranee had no intention of allowing her prey to escape, and, with a cruel vindictiveness that was truly Satanic, she instigated the Sepoys to break their pledged word and massacre them all. They fell upon the little band of victims and sabred or shot every man, woman, and child but one person, who escaped as by a miracle.

Thus cruelly and summarily did the Ranee of Jhansee take her revenge. Did she find it sweet? Were the shrieks of frightened, wounded women and children, and the groans of the dying, music to her ears? It does not seem possible; but this woman had never been taught a more satisfactory method of taking revenge. "An eye for an eye, and a tooth for a tooth," was the rule among the people of Hindoostan, and these atrocities which stain her character may, after all, be more attributable to her teachers and priestly advisers than to herself.

But whether her longing desire for revenge was sated or not, the deed was accomplished, and there was nothing to hinder her from re-occupying the position she had so unwillingly evacuated about three years before. She at once assumed the reins of Government, and, with great judgment and energy, began to arrange for the defense of the city, well knowing that the time would come when she would be called to a reckoning.

Supplies of men and provisions were gathered in from the province until she had an army of fourteen thousand men. For some reason Raja Rao Ramchunder had buried about twenty pieces of cannon in the fort. These were now disinterred and placed in position.

For a few months the Ranee had every thing her own way, but ere the year rolled round a retributive army, under Sir Hugh Rose, slowly but surely approached Jhansee.

Upon the 25th of April, 1858, the English opened fire upon the city. There could be but one result, but the struggle was a sharp one. The Hindoos fought with desperation, and showed so much skill in their firing of cannon that it was evident they had practiced considerably.

The batteries were largely worked by women, and they could be seen from the English lines as they hurried along, carrying ammunition to supply the guns.

There were three thousand men who defended the royal palace, and these were conspicuous for their bravery. The Ranee, and all her officers, soldiers, and women, evidently intended to make a *successful resistance*, but they were obliged to yield to superior force and valor.

On the second day the city was carried, and on the third the fort fell into the hands of the English. The Ranee, with about two thousand of her troops, fled from the city, and, having retreated a few miles, made another stand, and retained her position for a few days. On the 26th of May she was attacked and defeated, when she fled to Gwalior, where the rebels were still in power. She joined them with her few remaining men, and was hailed as an important accession ; but that city was shortly after retaken and re-occupied by the English.

With the remnant of her troops, the Ranee then fled toward the town of Sepree ; but she soon fell in with English troops, who must have seemed to her to be every-where. She tried to force her way through without an actual engagement, but finding it impossible, made a stand and gave battle. A sharp, decisive action ensued, and the cruel and ambitious, but brave, Ranee met her death upon the field, and her army was entirely destroyed.

We have not sketched the character and life of the Ranee of Jhansee in order to hold her up as a model of female excellence, but only to show her courage and energy. She possessed these qualities in an unusual degree, although, unhappily, her extreme ambition only rendered them the surer and swifter means of her ruin. But if this ambition had been directed by wise teachers toward noble and lofty aims, and if her heart and intellect had been warmed and purified by Christianity, what a power for good she would have been, and we can but hope that some such women may speedily be numbered among the ranks of enlightened native Christian women in India.

Apostles to the zananas are needed, as well as

laborers among the multitudes of women of the humbler ranks, right from among their Christianized countrywomen—women who will not count their ease, their property, nor their lives, dear unto themselves, so that they may but lead their sisters to Christ.

The Begum of Bhopal.

THE BEGUMS OF BHOPAL.

ABOUT three hundred and seventy miles south of Delhi lies the fertile province of Bhopal, which is now, and has been for some time, governed by a Queen, or Begum, as she is styled in the Hindoostanee language.

The province is north of the Vindhya Mountains and the Nerbudda river, but not far from them. It has about eight thousand nine hundred and sixty-four square miles, and a population of nine hundred and fifty thousand. It yields quite a large revenue, nearly one hundred thousand dollars of which is annually paid to the British Government to support a body of soldiers at the city of Sehore, where an English agent resides.

Dost Mahomed, the founder of the Bhopal family, came to India from Afghanistan in the reign of the Mogul king, Aurungzebe, into whose service he entered. This occurred near the close of the seventeenth century.

Soon after entering the Mogul service, Dost Mahomed was sent in command of a force to subjugate the province of Malwa, which joins Bhopal. He was successful, and received promotion for his services. Shortly after he married the daughter of a Hindoo chief, and, upon the death of his father-in-law, seized upon the family possessions. He thus became possessed of considerable wealth, which he employed in training his dependents in the use of arms, and fitting out independent expeditions against petty Hindoo rulers. He was, in fact, a Mahomedan *brigand!*

One of these chiefs, a Raja of some eminence, thought to make a friend of this powerful and unscrupulous marauder, and proposed an alliance with him. His overtures were accepted, and a treaty was concluded. Shortly after the Raja was threatened by trouble from another quarter, and was protected by his Mahomedan ally. His gratitude was great, and he made over the province and city of Bhopal to him and his heirs forever. He also asked him to take up his residence with him in his own fort. The unsuspicious Raja little knew what a serpent he was taking to his bosom. The Mahomedan was as false as his own prophet, and having secretly admitted a body of his savage warriors within the fort, soon made himself master of the place. This atrocious villainy is an illustration of the saying, that "bad men will not make good friends."

Dost Mahomed employed the remaining part of his life in constructing a high wall around the city of Bhopal and in building a fort. He died in 1723, and his heirs ruled in Bhopal until the close of the eighteenth century, when Hayat Mahomed Khan came to the throne, but was so utterly inefficient that the country would have fallen a prey to the Mahrattas had not Wazeer Mahomed Khan, the son of another branch of the family, opportunely come to Bhopal to render his aid.

This man was the founder of the present reigning family. He must have been a man of rare integrity and humility, for he suffered Hayat Mahomed Khan, and afterward his son, Ghos Mahomed Khan, both men of inferior abilities, to bear the name of Nuwab, while he continued to command the army and the State, and thus save both from destruction. It seemed often that the little province would be overrun by the myriad hosts of Mahratta robbers, and Wazeer Mahomed several times sought help from the British Government, which was refused. At length, in 1814, the powerful Mahratta general, Sindia, determined to conquer the hitherto victorious little State, and prepared to advance with an overwhelming force. Bhopal, as an independent Government, would soon have been extinct, and the sketches of our Begums would never have been written, had not the English Government at last interposed, and quietly but firmly intimated to the Mahratta that he must desist. Like a chained lion he must have felt when a power he dare not resist or disobey prevented him from taking possession of the tempting prey.

Wazeer Mahomed died in 1816, and the people, fully understanding that the real ruler had died, wholly ignored the weak Ghos Mahomed and his family, and placed Nazar Mahomed, the son of Wazeer Mahomed, upon the throne.

Very fortunately, Ghos Mahomed had a marriageable daughter whom the Nuwab married, and thus united the two branches of the family and settled the question of the dynasty incontestably.

The reign of this prince was, however, of short duration, as he was accidentally shot by his brother-in-law, Faujdar Mahomed Khan, a boy about eight years old. He left one daughter, Sikander Begum, who, by the advice of the English Government, was betrothed to her cousin, Muneer Mahomed, and he was appointed Nuwab. The widow of Nazar Mahomed was to be regent during the minority of the young Nuwab, but he was impatient to taste the sweets of authority, and rose in rebellion to depose the regent. He was soon defeated, and lost all chance of sitting upon the throne of Bhopal. He was obliged to resign his claim to the hand of the young Begum, and to retire into private life. The events that followed make it seem very probable that the regent, or, as she was called, the Kudsiah Begum, may have been to blame in the first instance. It is evident that she liked to be "dressed in a little brief authority" so well that she desired to prolong the situation.

Sikandar Begum was married to Jahangeer Mahomed Khan, a younger brother of her first betrothed.

and soon after the wedding festivities he was seized by the regent and placed in confinement. In 1837 he escaped, and, having gathered a body of adherents, appeared in arms against the regent. She, with all the State resources at her command, easily defeated him, and he was obliged to take refuge in a certain fort. This she besieged, and there was a fierce conflict and much loss of life; but the British Government could not allow this state of things to continue longer, and compelled the parties to come to an amicable adjustment of their difficulties.

It was agreed that the regent should retire into private life on a generous income, and that the Nuwab Jahangeer Mahomed Khan should take his position as ruler of Bhopal. He was duly installed, November, 1837, and the vexed nation hoped for a reign of peace. But, unfortunately, the Nuwab and his wife, Sikandar Begum, disliked each other excessively, and, as their differences increased continually, she left him and resided with her mother. This state of things continued for seven years, when the Nuwab died. He seems to have done his utmost to deprive his wife and daughter of their rightful heritage by leaving the throne to an illegitimate son in his will, but the great arbitrator of India, the powerful British Government, again stepped in, and placed Shah Jahan Begum, the daughter, upon the throne. Faujdar Mahomed Khan was appointed regent, but three years later he resigned, and the Sikandar Begum was appointed regent. This was her rightful position, and she soon showed how admirably she was fitted to occupy it. She found the finances in a very disorderly condition, and addressed herself at once to the task of arranging a thorough revenue system. She encouraged her subjects to improve their buildings and lands, and, in order that they might have confidence that their property rights would be respected, she personally attended to the administration of justice, and prevented, as far as possible, the extortions of under officers.

Her daughter was married in 1855 to the commander-in-chief of the State army, and it was settled that he should receive the honorary title of Nuwab, but that the young Begum should assume the reins of government upon becoming of age. But before this event occurred, her mother so endeared herself to the English Government by remaining a firm friend and ally, when friendship was especially precious, that the arrangement was not carried out.

The Sepoy Mutiny showed the English both their enemies and friends in strong relief, and among the latter was the Mahomedan queen. All around her English power was swept away like chaff before the wind From the surrounding cities weary, panting, white-faced fugitives came flying to Bhopal, from certain death to an uncertain refuge. But their fears were soon quieted by the kindness of their reception, and they were sent with a protecting escort to Hoshyungabad, a city on the Nerbudda, which was garrisoned with faithful Madras troops.

Meanwhile the zeal of the people of Bhopal in behalf of their religion was burning in their veins, and they longed to join in the Mahomedan battle-cry of "Deen, Deen," (Faith, Faith,) and in destroying the infidel English.

They saw the English agent and his friends, who were residing at the Court of Bhopal, go in and out in safety, and murmured that they were withheld from imbruing their hands in their blood. Murder was in their hearts, and they could not wholly restrain their tongues from giving expression to their thoughts. The Begum heard the muttering thunder, and hastened to send the agent and his suite to join the other refugees.

Soon an English army marched down into Central India, under Sir Hugh Rose, to put matters to rights again. The Begum of Bhopal was not afraid to meet her old allies, for she had acted a noble and wise part, and was sure of their commendation and gratitude. She now furnished supplies to the army, and also sent a body of her own troops to assist them.

At length the tornado had passed, the shattered fragments of power reunited, and the British Government had leisure to reward its friends. The Begum of Bhopal was made Grand Commander of the Order of the Star of India, an Order originated by the Prince Consort especially for Anglo-Indian civilians who should distinguish themselves, and for faithful Indian allies. Its motto is, "Heaven's Light our Guide." An addition was also made to her territories of a district which added about eighty thousand dollars per annum to her treasury.

The Shah Jahan Begum became of age some time in 1859, but her mother had reigned with so much wisdom and ability that neither the people nor the British Government would consent to her removal in order to make way for her daughter. It was settled, therefore, that she should rule for life, and that Shah Jahan Begum and her heirs should succeed her.

Happy and busy in her numerous and onerous labors, the Begum continued to rule until the end of 1863, when she left her daughter in charge of State affairs, and with her aged mother, the Kudsiah Begum, and her uncle, the aged Faujdar Mahomed Khan, with their suites of attendants, went on a pilgrimage to Mecca, the birthplace of Mahomed, and the goal of every true believer in the religion he founded.

This pilgrimage the Begum doubtless considered would be a fitting termination to her life, for, though so faithful a friend to the English, she was still a devout believer in the Mahomedan faith. She made all her arrangements with characteristic energy and thoroughness, and scrupulously performed the ceremonies enjoined upon pilgrims from the beginning to the end of the pilgrimage. A Moulvai who accompanied her was directed to keep a full diary of the progress of the journey, the impressions made upon the mind of the Begum, etc., so that this curious work, which has since been published, is in reality the Begum's own book.

Before starting she went through the prescribed ablutions and repeated two prayers, then read suitable verses from the "venerable Koran." Upon the day of departure she visited the tombs of her father and grandfather, and prayed for the repose of their spirits. She then prayed for all her relatives, and for all Mahomedans, and asked that a blessing might rest upon them on account of her pilgrimage, that their absolution and her own might be thereby secured, and that she might return in safety.

The Begum and her friends sailed from Bombay in January, 1864, in the ship "Indore," which had been chartered for them. They were accompanied as far as Jeddah by the English agent of Bhopal. Jeddah is situated about midway up the Red Sea, on the Arabian coast. Here all pilgrims disembark for Mecca, which is three day's march distant. Some of the religious ceremonies begin, however, before landing.

Right by the sea at Jeddah stands a high, bold mountain, called Yalamlam, the sighting of which is the signal for the pilgrims to assume the prescribed garments and vows. From this time they all leave their heads uncovered day and night, and abstain from using perfumes, killing animals, etc., for a certain portion of the pilgrimage.

The royal pilgrims landed at Jeddah on the 24th of January, and addressed themselves to the task of visiting all the holy places laid down in their plan. The Begum visited the tombs of several saints and prayed for their souls. Her mother, the Kudsiah Begum, visited the tomb of "our grandmother, the venerable Eve, the wife of the holy Adam," and, according to her custom, distributed alms freely. But she met with an ill return for her liberality, for when she left the shrine, a crowd of two or three hundred beggars, men, women, and children, besieged her so importunately that she nearly fainted, and was carried off with some difficulty by her attendants. It seems to be the gentle practice of these earnest beggars to attack people who are not liberal enough to please them, in the hope of gaining by violence what they failed to obtain by persuasion.

The Sikander Begum refrained from paying her respects at the tomb of our common "grandmother," being warned by her mother's experience. Jeddah is not a large city. It contains only eight mosques, the most celebrated of which is that of Zachariah. There is, of course, the Jama Musjid, or Clothes Mosque, and probably there are numerous calls upon its charities. They are very particular in this mosque to read the *khutba*, or prayer for the ruling powers, every Friday, which is the holy day of Mahomedans. The Imam, or governor of Jeddah, ascends the pulpit with the mace of office in his hands, and, with a shawl over his head, reads the appointed formula.

The Begum was not favorably impressed with Jeddah. She says of it, "Jeddah is a desolate-looking city, very dirty, and pervaded with unsavory odors. The atmosphere is damp, and there are no water-tanks of any size." While there she corresponded with the officials of Mecca—the Shareef and the Pasha—in regard to her journey to that city. It was settled that a brother of the Shareef, and Sulaiman Begh—that is, Prince Solomon, the son of the Pasha—should come nearly to Jeddah to meet her. This advance party of welcome is called the *Istiqbal,* and is customary in eastern countries when a visitor of distinction is expected, the distance of the meeting from the destination being proportioned to the rank of the guest.

The journey from Jeddah to Mecca was made upon Shagdaf camels. These camels carry two persons. There are open panniers, called kajawas, on either side of the animal, in which the passengers sit. The Shebree camel only carries one person, who sits upon a square saddle upon its back. At the first halt they met the brother of the Shareef and the son of the Pasha, with their retinues of fifty sowars, or mounted soldiers, each. The Shareef's brother was preceded by an Abyssinian, who wore a fur hat and had two small kettle-drums before him, upon which he was beating with both hands, and holding his horse's reins in his mouth. The Pasha's son, being of lower rank, was preceded by only *one* kettle-drum. They remained over night at this place, called Haddah, and next day went on to Bertoi, where they found two hundred foot soldiers waiting for them.

On the evening of the third day they entered the so-called holy and exalted city of Mecca by the "Bab-us-salam," or, "Gate of Peace." Just as they passed within the gate the muezzin's call to prayer sounded out from within the principal mosque, and the invitation, doubtless, met an enthusiastic response in the hearts of the royal pilgrim and her friends, and we can fancy the whole party falling upon their knees and presenting their petitions. Prayer over, the Begum went at once to the *Kaaba*, the holy house of God, built by Abraham himself! At the building called Abraham's House she read the prescribed prayers, and then performed the ceremony of the first *toaf*. This is done as follows: The pilgrims start from a certain black stone, which is set in gold and placed in a corner of the holy precincts, and make the circuit of the holy places within the Kaaba, meanwhile repeating verses of the Koran.

When they return to the stone they say, "Bism Allah Allahoo Akbar," (in the name of God, who alone is great,) and then kiss the stone. This is repeated seven times, the whole thing being termed a "toaf." The second toaf takes place after the *haj*, or pilgrimage, has been completed; and the third is performed after all other rules and obligations have been met, and the *hajees*, or pilgrims, are on the eve of departure. After completing this last toaf they drink of the water of Zam Zam, the holy well adjoining the Kaaba, then kiss the door of the building, and, walking backward, retire from the place.

There are in all one hundred holy places in Jeddah and Mecca, being mosques, mountains, wells, caves, and stones. The Mosque of Hosain is very holy, because Mahomed planted his standard upon the site where it stands on the day he captured Mecca.

The "Tongue of Stone" has the following tradition attached to it. Mahomed was once on his way to the Kaaba for prayer when Satan said to him, "Prayers are over, do not go," this tongue simultaneously appearing on a wall near by. The prophet, knowing it to be a temptation, replied, "I will go at once to the Kaaba, for I know that prayers are not over." There is another holy stone called the "Stone of Abraham." The pilgrims fill the hollow in the stone, which is said to be the impression of the foot of Abraham, with water from the well Zam Zam, and then drink the water from the hollow. Then prayers and verses from the Koran are read. The tradition of the stone is as follows: "When the holy Abraham, the friend of God, was building the Kaaba he built it as high as he could reach, and then prayed to God to enable him to build it still higher.

Immediately this stone was sent upon the back of a horse, called Burak, with directions that Abraham should stand upon it and thus complete the building. He obeyed, and as he continued to build, the stone, of its own accord, rose higher, and raised him on a level with the increasing height of the walls." It is not said how Abraham got down to earth again after finishing the walls.

The well "Zam Zam Shareef" is supposed to be particularly holy. When drinking of its water the pilgrims always stand, and ask a blessing before, and return thanks after, drinking. Bathing in this water secures great blessings; and muslin dipped in it, and dried without wringing, is made holy, and is purchased by the wealthy to serve as shrouds. If a few drops of this water can be put into the mouth of a dying person they esteem it a great blessing, and it is carried home in bottles by pilgrims for this purpose. The greatest attraction of all is, however, the sukh-ul-lail, or house where Mahomed was born.

The Sikandar Begum went through these minute and tiresome ceremonies apparently without flinching, although her annoyances were not few. Many of these arose from the rapacity of the religious mendicants which throng the city, and others by her ignorance of the etiquette to be observed with the officials. At length an agent was furnished from either side to arrange all forms to be observed between them. The aged Kudsiah Begum paid visits to the zenanas of the Shareef and Pasha, and was treated with great respect. The Sikandar Begum then sent her deputy to arrange for her to make similar visits, and, according to Indian custom, he made an offering of a few guineas to both the officers.

The Shareef accepted them, saying, "I accept these out of respect for the etiquette of your country, although it is not the custom here;" but the Pasha declared it was a very improper and disgraceful custom, and did not take the money.

The Begum's account of her visit is most interesting. She says, "I went on foot to the Shareef's house, where I was met by three slaves, who requested me to go into the zenana, which I proceeded to do, they leading the way. At the first step of the stair-case to the zenana some slaves were stationed; three or four steps higher were some female Egyptians, servants of the mother and sisters of the Shareef. These women placed their hands under my arms and assisted me up the steps. Several steps higher was one of the Shareef's wives, and a little higher another wife, then beyond stood his mother. As she met me she put my hand in hers, and then, putting her face against both sides of my face and neck, ended with kissing me lightly on the lips.

"An hour afterward some slaves came to me to say that the Shareef would, with my permission, come into the zenana. I replied, 'It is the Shareef's own house;' meaning, 'of course, he can do as he pleases.' I was sitting with his mother and wives and conversing with the former. The Shareef has seven wives, four of whom I saw. Of these, two were Georgians, very handsome, and beautifully dressed, being, one might say, literally covered with diamonds from head to foot. Their heads were encircled with a wreath composed of jewels, and when they moved or talked the sparkling effect was very pretty. Underneath this diadem they wore on their heads very small fine handkerchiefs, such as English ladies carry in their hands; these were thickly embroidered with jewels and tied in a coquettish way. Altogether, in face, height, and beauty of limbs, these two Georgians were as perfect women as one could wish to see. The dress of one was composed of black satin, and that of the other of lilac satin embroidered with stars.

"The third wife was an Arabian, and had regular features. The fourth was an Abyssinian. Those wives only who have borne children to the Shareef are allowed to sit in his presence; while those who have no family are compelled to stand, with their hands put together.

"When the Shareef came into the zanana the four wives and the mother rose respectfully, and I advanced a few steps to meet him. After the Shareef was seated I made my offering, and then followed the usual complimentary speeches. Having inquired after my health, the Shareef asked, 'How far is Bhopal from here?' I replied, 'It is the paradise of India; your highness should pay it a visit.' The Shareef laughed, and said, "My home is the kaaba." After this the wives and mother, having again made their obeisance, sat down in the background. Some Georgians and Africans who were in attendance now brought in cups of coffee and pomegranate sherbet, and others the rose-water and incense. Just as it is the fashion in India to give attar and rose-water, so it is the custom in Mecca to fumigate the guests with sweet-scented incense."

The Begum also mentions her visit to the Pasha, but does not enter so minutely into particulars. She says, in regard to visiting his zanana: "I was received by the ladies in the same manner as at my visit to the Shareef's family." Her remarks on Mecca, "the Exalted," are inserted, slightly abbreviated: "It is wild and melancholy looking, and has a dreary, repulsive aspect. Sometimes the weather is cold, then again extremely hot, in consequence of which there is a prevalence of inflammatory diseases and of catarrh. The nights are very cool and pleasant, the sky remaining perfectly clear, and the moonlight is magnificent, but an hour before sunrise it begins to be as hot as in the day time. Often there are high winds and thunder and lightning, but very little rain. There is not a single tree in the whole city, and vegetables are scarce ; but plentiful supplies of these and of fruits are brought in regularly from a neighboring city. The people have dreadfully harsh voices, and are not well-formed, except their heads and shoulders, which are handsome. The women have even greater muscular strength than the men, and are large-made and noisy. The people take a great quantity of food, as much as five or six pounds daily. The strength of the men is such that they are able to lift a weight of twelve mans, (nine hundred and sixty pounds,) whereas in India no one carries more than three mans, (two hundred and forty pounds,) and this burden they will carry alone to the top of a high house. Their complexions vary, some being very dark, and others quite fair, but most of them have light brown or golden hair. In character the majority are miserly, violent-tempered, hard-hearted, and covetous, and they are both awkward and stupid."

The Begum used her eyes freely while in Mecca, and her extreme openness of speech somewhat displeased the officials. She thought the sanitary arrangements were very imperfect, and that the thirty lacs of rupees (one million five hundred thousand dollars) per annum, which are allowed by the Sultan of Turkey to keep up the holy places at Mecca and Medina, were not properly expended. She remarked one day, in the hearing of an under officer, that there was no cleanliness in the city, and the arrangements at the shrines were not good ; and, with almost incomprehensible simplicity, added: "Now, if the Sultan of Turkey would give *me* these thirty lacs, I would make arrangements for the government of Bhopal to be carried on by my son-in-law and daughter, and you would see what a state of order and cleanliness *I* would keep the august cities in, and what arrangements *I* would make for the proper maintenance of the holy shrines, so that the Sultan would find out that dishonest people had been diverting his money from its legitimate uses, and had not kept a single thing in order; *while I, in a few days, would effect a complete reformation.*"

This exceedingly plain speech was, of course, reported straightway to the Shareef and Pasha, and must have incensed them greatly; and it is a wonder that the Begum got off with being told by the Pasha on his next visit that "Some people come on the pilgrimage in a spirit of humility, and not with their heads lifted up; many others who are obstinate and designing also come, and what do they gain by it?"

The Begum says of this, "Altogether, I felt convinced that the Pasha was angry with me for my speech. If he had been a man of liberal views he would have been rather pleased than otherwise, and would have asked me to explain what arrangements I thought were required."

Alas! short-sighted Begum! Did she expect a man enjoying a monopoly by which he could enrich himself to court inquiry, and of a woman? The Begum did not visit Medina, but went directly back to Bhopal after seven or eight weeks' sojourn in Arabia, resumed the cares of government, and gave her attention to the welfare of her subjects. She had always encouraged educational efforts in her dominions, and she now gave considerable attention to the establishing of schools both for boys and girls.

The Sikandar Begum died on the 18th of October, 1868, having governed Bhopal with great firmness, and with an energy quite unoriental, for twenty-one years.

Her daughter, Shah Jahan Begum, was duly placed upon the throne. She was also a widow, her husband having died the previous year, leaving her with one child, a daughter eleven years old, called the Sultan Jahan Begum. The following article, which appeared in one of the leading English newspapers in India in 1869, shows the estimation in which both the present and the late Begum are held :—

"The lady who at present sits on the throne of Bhopal bids fair to rival her mother's fame as an administrator. During a reign of twenty-one years the late Begum had materially improved the condition of the State by encouraging education, by bringing waste land under cultivation, to the benefit of her subjects as well as of her treasury; by abolishing monopolies, by organizing an efficient police, and by reducing the public debt. But for some time past, owing to failing health, her pilgrimage to Mecca, and other causes, she had not been able to make a tour through her dominions, and the consequence was that misrule on the part of local officials was not infrequent. It has been the first care of the present Begum, after the days of mourning for her mother were ended, personally to investigate all abuses. For more than three months during the hottest season of the year she has been in camp, moving from district to district, so that every one who had a grievance might have full opportunity of getting it remedied.

"Before starting she issued a proclamation to the effect that she had reason to believe there had been oppression in various quarters, and that therefore she summoned every one who had any complaint against any of her officers, high or low, whether then in office or already retired, to attend and represent his case. The invitation has been generally accepted, and the inquiry has ended in much good both to the State and to individuals. Public servants who were found to be old and infirm have been pensioned; those who were convicted of fraudulent transactions, of receiving bribes, of exactions, or of selling justice, have been dismissed and punished; and, whenever it was possible, any sum which had been taken, over and above what was due, has been refunded. The weights of shopkeepers have been examined, and such as were proved to be deficient were set straight, the owners of them at the same time being fined. Dilapidated buildings belonging to the State have been repaired, encamping grounds have been planted round with trees, tanks have been deepened, and wells dug. In short, whatever a patient hearing of petitions, and a judicious expenditure of money, could do, has been done.

"The example of such devotion, energy, and loyalty as characterize the past and present Begums of Bhopal, is as rare as it is praiseworthy."

The accompanying picture* is a portrait of the present Begum as she appeared on the sixteenth of November, 1872, in the vice-regal tent in Bombay, where she also was invested with the Order of the Star of India. The Secretary of State presented her with the badge and star. The cloak, which was too long for her short figure, was placed upon her shoulders by the minister of finance, and the gold collar by the viceroy. She then shook hands with all present who had received the Order, and was then required to sign the promises connected with it. Her oldest attendant then unfurled the banner of Bhopal, trumpets were sounded, and the secretary of the Order proclaimed her highness' titles, which concluded the ceremony.

It is to be hoped that this intelligent and energetic Queen may turn her attention yet more specifically

* See portrait facing page 153.

to the promotion of female education and elevation. Her own example must be an inspiration to her countrywomen, and with the means of education furnished them, we would undoubtedly see the females of Bhopal taking advanced ground among the women of Hindoostan.

THE WOMEN OF INDIA.

Hindoo Women.

IT is evident, from the foregoing sketches, that the position held by Hindoo women in former ages was much higher than it is at present. Hindoos themselves claim this to be so, and direct attention to their ancient laws in regard to women to prove their statement. They also claim to have been compelled to adopt their present custom of keeping their women in seclusion in order to protect them from the lawlessness of the Mahomedan conquerors of Hindoostan, and that in consequence of this practice they also ceased to educate them.

The influence of Mahomedan opinions and companionship was felt more especially in Bengal and Northern India, and in those parts of the country high caste Hindoo women are kept in stricter seclusion now than in other portions of the land ; and this fact seems to corroborate the theory of the Hindoos in regard to the reason of the change in their customs.

In the Rajpootana States especially considerable liberty seems to have been enjoyed by females, and they were evidently educated, and taught to think, and even act, for themselves. They were expected to rule nations and lead armies to battle in cases of emergency, and were instructed in all matters which in such emergences would be necessary for them to know.

The same is also true of the great Mahratta nation of South-western India, who have never kept their women in strict seclusion. One writer says of them: "The females both of the Brahmin and Sudra Mahratta's have, generally speaking, when their husbands are princes and chiefs, great influence, and mix, not only by their power over individuals, but sometimes personally, in affairs of State. If married to men of rank they have usually a distinct provision and estate of their own, and enjoy as much liberty as they can desire, seldom if ever wear a vail, and give feasts and entertainments on births, marriages, and particular anniversaries. They are usually instructed in reading, writing, and mathematics, and are taught sewing. The management of the horse always constitutes part of their education, which is directed to qualify them for the duties to which they are liable."

The barbarous practice of suttee, or widow-burning, which prevailed so generally among the Hindoos when the English began to dwell in India, over two hundred years ago, seems to have been a corruption that gradually crept into their religious observances, the reasons and rules for which were incorporated in some of their later sacred books. This dreadful practice was, however, the legitimate fruit of the corrupt tree of idolatry.

It is evident, from Hindoo laws, that suttee was only to be voluntarily observed, as provision is made in them for the maintenance of widows, and men are enjoined to treat them with respect, and are held up to obloquy, as worthy of being classed with thieves and robbers, if they withhold the rightful property of widows from them. Suttee was officially forbidden throughout British Indian territory by Lord William Bentinck, governor general of India, on the 14th of December, 1829.

A case of attempted suttee, which occurred a month or two before this time, is mentioned in the "Life of Sir Henry Lawrence," and as the laws regulating the observance of the rite are mentioned, I quote it entire :—

"It was attempted on the bank of the river Ganges, near the fort of Allahabad, and was defeated by the humanity, courage, and wisdom of two Englishmen, Mr. George Brown, of the civil service, and the Rev. Mr. Mackintosh, a Baptist missionary. These two good men, hearing what was going on, repaired to the spot, forced their way up to the funeral pyre, and producing the sacred books of the Hindoos, informed the officiating pundits and Brahmins that they would allow nothing that was not according to the letter of the Hindoo law. To this the pundits could not object, and the result was that—

"1. No oil or other inflammable substance was allowed to be poured over the wood.

"2. The widow was led to the Ganges and there immersed, so that her garments were dripping wet instead of dry and ready to ignite.

"3. The Brahmins were forbidden either to bind the widow down to the pile, or give her intoxicating drugs. The sacrifice must be voluntary, or not at all.

"So the widow was left unbound and in her senses. No priest was allowed to fire the pile. The books declare that the widow must do this herself. These points having been insisted on, the trembling widow, with wet clothes clinging round her, mounted the fatal pile, and worked herself up so far as to apply the torch. But as the flames began to rise and climb from log to log and dart their horrid tongues at the poor widow, she became restless and excited. First she drew up one foot, then the other, then gazed wildly round upon the howling priests, then stood upright and danced and shrieked with pain, and at last, unable to bear it longer, leaped out of the fire. On this the Englishmen stepped forward and took her under the protection of British law. Of course her family would have nothing to say to her, so her humane rescuers set her up in a small shop in the bazar, and whenever either of them passed, she used to run out into the street and make salams, crying out, 'That's the good sahib that saved my life!'

This scene occurred only forty-six years ago, and yet British supremacy in India dates from the battle of Plassey, in 1757."

According to Marshman, the first effort to suppress the practice of suttee was made by Mr. George Udny, and Dr. Carey, the indefatigable Baptist missionary of Serampore. They presented an address on the subject to Lord Wellesley, governor general of India; but he was just leaving the country, and could not act in the matter. He recorded a minute, however, in favor of abolishing the rite.

The sudder, or chief court, did not favor the abolition of the usage, but endeavored to regulate it; and the Bombay Government, taking the same course, even went so far as to employ an English official to construct the funeral pyre when the rite of suttee was to be performed, in order to do it in such a manner as to allow of the escape of the widow should her fortitude give out. But it soon became evident that such partial measures only tended to legalize and increase the practice. Nevertheless, some of the most distinguished Indian civilians thought the rule of *religious toleration*, to which they considered English authority owed its stability, would be violated if they should deprive Hindoos of the sacred and precious privilege of burning their widows. Many other officials, however, took a more Christian view of the subject, and urged the peremptory prohibition of suttee, and, of course, the few missionaries in the country were of the same opinion, and did all in their power to influence the public mind in regard to the question.

The Court of Directors of the East India Company (in London) at last placed the matter in the hands of the governor general, and it was at this juncture that Lord William Bentinck went out to India in that capacity. He determined to take the question up at once, and decide it in the fear of God. He met with violent opposition, but three fourths of the civilians were in favor of "positive prohibition." There were two eminent orientalists then in India, Dr. Horace Wilson and Mr. (afterward Sir) William Macnaghten. The former was a great friend of the Hindoos; not a friend to their true progress, however, for he strenuously opposed the suppression of suttee, and declared that "the practice could not be abolished without doing violence to the conscientious belief of every order of Hindoos; that it would be a dire interference with their religion, etc."

Mr. Macnaghten, on the contrary, warmly advocated its abolition. "Let the Hindoo," he said, "believe in his three hundred and thirty millions of gods until it may please the Almighty to reclaim him from his idolatry, but let him not immolate thousands of helpless females on the altar of fanaticism."

The result of the inquiries instituted by Lord

William Bentinck was so favorable to the immediate abolition of the inhuman and atrocious rite that he, with his two counselors, Mr. Butterworth Bayley and Sir Charles Metcalfe, on the 14th of December, 1829, passed the celebrated regulation which "declared the practice of suttee illegal, and punishable by the criminal courts as culpable homicide;" * and shortly after Dr. Carey, who held the appointment of government translator at the time, had the privilege one Sunday of putting the order against suttee into the Bengalee language, and, knowing that a day's delay might be fatal to scores of women, did not deem it a sacrilegious occupation for that day.

Since that time suttee has gradually died out, until attempts to perform it are very rare. Occaally a case is reported to Government. One such occurred within the last year; but suttee, as a practice, is among the things that were, and faithful Hindoo wives have to content themselves with the less heroic teachings of the sacred book of the Sikhs: "They are not suttees who perish in the flames; O Nanuk, suttees are they who die of a broken heart!" The meaning of the word "suttee" is true or faithful.

Such a change has been wrought among the people by the light of education and Christianity that probably, if English rule were to be withdrawn, the practice of suttee would never again be allowed. Educated Hindoos are heartily ashamed of these atroci-

* See Marshman's "History of India," vol. ii, page 399.

ties, and speak of them as deprecatingly as we do. The practice of murdering female infants prevailed both among the wild aboriginal tribes and the more civilized and educated Hindoos. In 1789 the English Resident in Benares made the discovery that it was prevalent among the Rajpoots; and in 1800, when the same gentleman was appointed to Bombay, he instituted inquiry upon the subject among the Rajpoots in the west, and ascertained that in two provinces at least three hundred helpless babes were murdered annually! In a territory about seven hundred miles in extent there were every year twenty thousand victims! The little creatures were either starved or drugged with opium by their unnatural parents.

It could not be ascertained that there was any *religious* origin of this horrible practice, but it seemed to have been taken up on account of the great expense of weddings and the insane pride of caste, which made it impossible for parents to marry their daughters except in their own tribe. This they might not always be able to accomplish if they had many daughters, and they considered it very disgraceful to have a daughter enter her teens unmarried.

The expense of a wedding, too, was enormous, in consequence of the inordinate feasting of guests and feeing of priests, bards, etc., the presents to friends, and the dowry of the bride. All these things were required by their senseless customs, so that even if husbands for his daughters could be found within his tribe, a large number of them would ruin a man of moderate fortune.

When the prevalence of infanticide came to the knowledge of the English officials they at once undertook its suppression. They despaired of effecting this by force, but endeavored to convince native chiefs of the enormity of the sin, and succeeded in making them sign agreements to renounce it themselves, and to discourage it by expelling from caste any persons who should afterward practice it. But many of the chiefs broke their word almost immediately, and it has only been by persistent effort on the part of English officials that this practice has been generally given up.

In 1849 the subject was discussed in the Punjab, where it was found to prevail among the Sikhs. Lord Dalhousie, the governor general of India, convened a durbar, or reception, in the city of Umritser, at the same time that a popular festival of the Sikhs was held. It was largely attended by the Hindoo, Sikh, and Mahomedan nobility. The chief commissioner of the Punjab addressed the assembled chieftains on the inhumanity of the practice, and the necessity for its suppression. The chiefs were deeply impressed, and solemnly promised to faithfully carry out any plans that the governor general and chief commissioner might inaugurate to effect the desired object. Committees were appointed to draw up a scale for the expense of weddings, which was accepted by the chiefs and established throughout their dominions. The Maharajah of Cashmere was one of the most zealous promoters of this good work.

In this way in various parts of the great country the people were brought to see the heinousness of infanticide and to renounce it; but the Government still keeps a constant watch upon them, and punishes with severity all persons found guilty of perpetrating the dreadful crime.

We find Hindoo women, then, are freed from the most atrocious wrongs they have had to bear in former ages, and our sympathy need not be stirred by the tales of horror that fifty years ago led Christian women to go to the far East and labor for their benighted and oppressed sisters. But the spirit of heathenism is that of tyranny, and we find many things in the condition of females in India yet that seem to us wrong and degrading. Some things, undoubtedly, *are* so, while others are not really so, considering the state of society there.

Women of the lower classes go about freely. We see them daily. They come to our houses, to the hospitals when sick, or, if unable to do so, are attended at their homes. They go about the streets, and pursue their avocations, and visit each other at will. The women of the higher classes often go out from their homes, but always in palanquins or other covered vehicles, from whose loop-holed curtains they can see without being seen. When their husbands become acquainted with missionaries and English families they often allow their wives to pay visits at their houses, trusting to their courtesy that due precautions will be taken to prevent their being seen by men.

There has doubtless been, and still is, much suffering among this class in sickness, as their customs forbid them from being attended by male physicians. This prejudice, however, is slowly but surely being removed, and medical missionaries are now sometimes, in extreme cases, called to see high-caste ladies. Nevertheless, female physicians will always find a wide field for usefulness in India, and can, if actuated by the true missionary spirit, by means of their medical skill, open the door for evangelistic labor in many localities where it would otherwise remain closed for years.

It seems to us that Hindoo women occupy a menial position, because they are not allowed to eat with their husbands or the male members of the family. But they do not so regard it. It is simply "their custom;" their fathers did so and they do the same.

Under the patriarchal system the households become very large. All the sons bring their wives home. They occupy rooms forming a quadrangle around an open court-yard. Here, or on the veranda, the food is brought when cooked. Some of the women look after the children, while others serve out the food to the men, who, when they have eaten, betake themselves to the genial occupation of "drinking the hookah," that is, *smoking* by drawing the smoke through the little reservoir of water attached to every eastern pipe. The men thus happily disposed of, the women and children have the whole field to themselves, and enjoy their meals at their leisure.

After the women have eaten, some of them also smoke; but, as a rule, they chew *pan* instead. Pan (*a* pronounced like *a* in father) is composed of a small piece of betel-nut, a clove or two, cardamom seed, and shell lime, wrapped in a pungent leaf and pinned together by a thorn. It is prepared for the market and brought in daily by the basketful. The juice of the pan is very red, and it gives the mouth a very singular appearance, not so repulsive, however, as does the chewing of tobacco, a practice which I have never known heathen to indulge in.

The elder women are highly venerated, as they are usually very strict in their religious observances, and their influence upon the household counsels is very great.

Many young women are kept from learning to read by their superstitious conservatism; and many an enlightened young man is kept from openly becoming a Christian on account of the horror and aversion with which his aged mother or grandmother would look upon his conduct.

Hindoo women are very devoted to their faith. They generally worship the goddesses, most of whom are said to be incarnations of Parbutee, the wife of Shiva, the destroyer. A particular one is chosen as the household guardian. In the Himalayas they pay great respect to Nynee Debee, the little idol whose *spirit* is supposed to have her home in the gigantic rocks which overhang the lake of Nynee Tal. The paharins, or hill women, send out their little girls, when just old enough to run about, to gather orchids and lilies of the valley, the fragrant clematis, the scattered flowers of the gorgeous rhododendrons, and many other blossoms of plant or tree that deck the mountain sides, to lay before the hideous stone idol in the little temple at the head of the lake.

Merry seasons for Hindoo women of all classes are the numerous festivals, when the deeds of the avatars, or incarnations of the deity, are celebrated, the festivals of the seasons, and the great annual melas on the banks of the Ganges. Hundreds of thousands gather at different points along the sacred "Gunga," and spend several days in traffic and visiting; then on the "last great day" they rush in surging masses into the river for the grand *wash* that shall cleanse them from the sins of the preceding year. This is the great event of the year to Hindoo women, when they can emerge from behind the curtain and take a good look at the world.

But this is only one side of the picture. They are slaves of the most puerile superstitions. They dread the curse of a Brahmin more than death itself. They are terrified at scores of natural events, and have a constant abject dread of evil that may happen to them or their children, and wear charms, and make offerings to avert it. They are, in short, utter strangers to a faith that gives rest to the soul. "The way of peace have they not known." No sweet trust in God and bright anticipations of heaven cheer them in the bereavements and sicknesses of life, and when death comes it is truly a "leap in the dark."

Although it is not customary for Hindoos to have several wives, yet they often take a second wife, and unhappiness in the family often results from this practice. They are betrothed in childhood, and if the boy die before the marriage is completed, the little girl is pronounced a widow, and, like those who are widowed after marriage, must remain single through the remainder of her life. She is debarred from wearing the numerous ornaments that delight heathen women: the ear and nose-jewels, the necklets and armlets, bracelets and anklets, and even the toe-rings, whose tiny bells "make a tinkling as they go." She can no longer attire herself in the bright-hued muslins and the beautifully embroidered dresses of rich and delicate fabrics in which, as a wife or expected bride, she was accustomed to be arrayed. She must wear coarse, white garments, and must occupy herself in the performance of household labor, and in caring for the welfare of her husband's family. She is often looked upon as a burden, and her state is most solitary and pitiable. This is not, however, always the case. There is as much difference in the social atmosphere of Hindoo families as among the families of civilized lands.

Since missionary ladies have reached the zenanas, many of this class have seemed particularly interested in their teaching, and there have been a few instances where they have, in spite of the threats of their relations, embraced Christianity. Of course they had to leave their homes and come to the missionaries for protection. They became teachers, and thus helped to spread the knowledge of Christ among their countrywomen. Such cases are, however, rare. When men find it so difficult to break away from the fetters of caste and family ties, it is not strange that women find such barriers insurmountable. A widow may more easily do it than others, but even she leaves all that has been the world to her for a strange faith and new friends.

Still we need not be discouraged in our labors among Hindoo women. Even if the barriers to professing their faith be insurmountable at first, they can have the peace and comfort that result from its possession, and will be prepared to assist and sympathize with their husbands, sons, and brothers who may be drawn toward Christianity, and ultimately to join with them in openly professing Christ.

Education and missionary labor have prevailed to so much greater extent among men than women that at present the latter are positive hinderances to the spread of the Gospel, but they will not be slow to appreciate its excellence when they become acquainted with its teachings. The tender, compassionate Saviour, who could when weary and hungry forget his fatigue and his wants in showing the way of life to a poor sinful woman, and who welcomed little children to his arms, will be recognized by them as just the Saviour and friend they need. There are many women in India who have come out from among the heathen and openly profess faith in Christ; and doubtless many others hope for salvation through him, although unable to join his people openly.

MAHOMEDAN WOMEN.

Among the Mahomedans we find a more vigorous type of womanhood than among Hindoos. Their women are not superior intellectually, but their superior faith gives them more hopefulness, and a more cheerful outlook upon the present and the future. Their prayers and alms are to please a holy and gracious God, instead of being offered to propitiate demon-like goddesses, and to avert their evil designs toward them. Many of them are taught to read, and their position in the household is more independent than among Hindoos, although women of the better classes are not allowed to go about unvailed or alone.

A sufee, or sanctified Mahomedan, who was once employed as my teacher, graciously remarked one day that it was evident to him that American women were gifted with intellects equal to the men; as he had known several who learned the Hindoostanee language as readily as their husbands. I asked him if he considered the women of his own nation to be intellectually inferior to the men. He replied, with true oriental circumlocution, "We certainly suppose women to be somewhat inferior to men; they *are* so physically, no doubt, and as to their minds, perhaps we do not give them a fair chance to show what they are capable of; on the whole, I think we rank them as high as men, *only a little less!*" I asked him if he was sure about their physical inferiority, and pointed him to the hill women, who carry as heavy burdens as the men.

He then remarked that he had a very clever wife. She took entire charge of his household expenses, kept all the money, and arranged the marriages of their children. "She is also very intelligent," he continued, "she converses readily upon many subjects; but then you see, madam, she has had the benefit of *my companionship all these years!*" He looked the personification of conscious wisdom as he spoke.

The lesson of the day was on the same subject. The book I was reading was a Mahomedan story designed to benefit women, and the lesson was a father's letter to his daughter, who was about to be married. He cautions her to beware of ever considering herself her husband's equal, since God had not only directed that woman's sphere should be lower than man's, but had also given her less understanding. Above all, he cautions her against ever trying to force her husband to do as *she* wishes, and here the *man* as well as the father is stirred within him, and he writes, "God has made man a *tiger*, and it will be impossible to conquer him!" He probably believed kindness is more effectual in taming wild animals, man included, than force. As his daughter, an intelligent, educated woman, was about to marry an obstinate, conceited dunce, at her father's behest, these counsels were doubtless well-timed.

SIKH WOMEN.

There is another class or sect of people in the north-west of India who are, from the very peculiarities of their faith, better prepared to receive the Gospel than others. They are called Sikhs. The word Sikh is the root of the verb *sikhna*, to learn, and means in this connection the instructed people.

Their founder, a man by the name of Nanuk, lived about the close of the fifteenth century. When a boy he attracted by his intelligence the attention of a Mahomedan moulvai, or priest, who had set his heart upon devising some scheme to unite Hindoos and Mahomedans in the bonds of a common faith. He educated this boy according to his own peculiar views, and had the satisfaction of seeing him arrive at man's estate fully imbued with the idea of founding a universal religion. The doctrine he promulgated was that worship was due to God alone, but the form of worship was immaterial. Caste distinctions were abolished.

The Sikhs flourished during the sixteenth and seventeenth centuries, and became a numerous and warlike people. They dwelt mostly in the Punjab, but a small and rather inferior portion of them called the Mazhabee Sikhs, eventually settled in the province of Rohilkund.

The Mazhabee Sikhs are rather nomadic in their habits, and are a rough, uncultivated people, but from the opening of the missions of the Methodist Episcopal Church in Rohilkund in the beginning of 1859, they have heard the Gospel gladly. At their request, the missionaries visited one of their villages before they had even procured a house for their own families. A large number of Sikhs—men, women, and children—gathered to welcome them, and to hear the Gospel message. Many consistent, earnest Christians have been raised up among them, and they are gradually becoming elevated and enlightened by means of schools and the constant labors of missionaries.

From the beginning of this work the Sikh women have been particularly interested in Christianity, and have received it quite as readily as the men. One bright girl about ten years of age, whose parents had become Christians, requested the missionary to baptize her too, as she was resolved to be a Christian. Her friends thought she had better wait awhile, but her urgency carried the day. She soon learned to read, and has ever since been engaged in teaching, or laboring in some way for the good of her countrywomen She is now, and has been for nearly four years, working as a medical Bible reader, and is very acceptable and useful both as a doctor and a Scripture reader. Many others are also worthy of mention and commendation.

The dress of the Sikhs was prescribed by their founder. It is almost wholly of dark blue cotton goods, in which the women especially look very ugly. They put their hair up very high on their heads, over which the dark blue chadar or shawl is worn. Their skirts are rather short, and their whole appearance very ungainly. The expression of their features, too, is rather dull and uninteresting. But even among this apparently unpromising class many, bright capable women have been found, who only needed the hope-inspiring influence of Christianity to waken them into moral and intellectual vigor.

In visiting among all classes of Hindoostanee women in the hope of doing them good, great tact and kindness are necessary. It is strange how quick they are to detect any rudeness in foreigners, even when they indulge in it themselves. They often become strongly attached to those who visit them, and are kind and sympathetic in their manners toward them, and the days on which they expect these visits are looked forward to as pleasant spots in their uneventful lives.

I have often been struck with the evident care that had been taken to have the rooms tidied up, and the women dressed neatly, so that we could sit down together and pursue our studies and conversation without interruption. Often, too, I have been greeted with the remark, "We have been watching for you for a long time; we thought that you would have come earlier;" and once when I waited past the hour I had promised to visit a family so that the sun might lose something of its fiery heat, a dear little boy, about five years old, was sent across a field to the little rest-house where we were staying to ask if I would not come soon. Very happy and proud was the little fellow when he was permitted to lead me back to the waiting company of women. A year after, when I again visited the place, the little son, of whom the mother was so fond and proud, and on whom the father's hopes were placed, had died, and I found sorrow and darkness where, a year previous, there was such a bright and joyous household. And yet the angel of life, as well as the angel of death, had visited the dwelling. A lovely little female infant smiled in the mother's arms, but very faint was the response on the mother's face. I said to her, in answer to some despairing remark she made, "It is not because God is angry with you that he took your darling boy; see, he has sent a little daughter to comfort you." She answered, "Should he give me *twelve* the vacant place in my heart would yet remain unfilled." I tried to cheer the poor stricken mother with the thought that her boy was taken away from all trouble and sin. No weary pilgrimage for him that his sins might be expiated, but, while innocent of actual transgression, he had been taken to a holy, happy heaven. I told her of the comforting thoughts Christians had at such times, and of the happy prospect of meeting our loved ones again, and dwelling forever with them in the presence of the Lord. She listened eagerly, and seemed to obtain a glimpse of the bright future opened up to the Christian through faith in Christ; but she recollected herself with a sigh, and replied wearily, "What can we know of such things; the future is all hidden from our eyes." *She* was a Hindoo, and *her* religion did not hold out such blessed hopes. Her mind was full of vague ideas of the transmigration of souls until they should become lost in the Deity. *Her boy* was lost to her forever. She never rallied from this depression of mind, but pined away for a few months and died.

Much pains are usually taken to show a missionary lady great respect. If the family can boast of a chair, it is brought and placed on a rug for the visitor; but if they have no chair, perhaps a low seat, made of bamboo and cord, called a morha, is brought, or she is requested to seat herself on a charpoy, or low bedstead, covered with woven cord and, perhaps, a rug, and they think it very odd that she does not draw her feet upon the bed as well. "O, how *can* you let your feet hang down?" they say; "don't they ache?" They are answered with one of their own idioms, "It is our custom," and are silenced if not convinced.

Once I visited a family where they had none of the above-mentioned conveniences; but they spread several tanned hides of the spotted deer upon the floor of the veranda, and we all sat down upon them. This time I was obliged to sit in true oriental fashion, whether I would or not.

Let not any one infer, however, that our eyes behold only the pleasant things of Indian household life. Far from it. Sights most repulsive meet us on every hand in the hot, filthy streets and habitations of a native city. Horses, cows, and donkeys are often kept in close proximity to the dwellings, and there are many other customs that are very unpleasant to us. The children are allowed to run about with very little clothing, and in far from a tidy state. The invalids of the family are very minute in explaining to visitors the exact nature of the diseases from which they suffer, and one's sympathies are often strongly excited by the exhibition of fearful and incurable sufferings.

As far as possible we persuade native women whom we visit to dispense with their custom of making offerings, as far as we are concerned. It is not expected that visitors will *receive* these gifts unless they intend to make a present in return, and if, through ignorance of this etiquette, they should accept what is pressed upon them and then not make quite as valuable a present in return, great offense would be taken. As a rule, we are seldom offered any thing of value after we become acquainted with a family, unless they consider themselves highly obliged by some kindness shown them, and wish to show their gratitude. They usually bring cardamom-seeds, almonds, raisins, pieces of cocoanut, and *pan* to us just before we leave, and we take something from the plate just to please them.

They are not always the only learners on these occasions. *We* often receive lessons on various subjects by having the "way that ithers see us" brought to our notice. An English lady once made an unexpected call upon some wealthy Hindostanee ladies, and found them richly dressed and bejeweled. She remarked to them, "How can you be to so much trouble in dressing and putting on all this jewelry when you do not go into society?" One of them answered, "Why, we wear our ornaments for our *husbands*. For whom do English ladies wear jewels and rich dresses?" Quite likely, in describing this scene to her liege lord afterward the Hindoostanee lady added, "And when I asked the Mem Sahib that question she ate her breath and remained silent."

We find stereoscopes and pictures of great use in zanana work. Short stories and explanations of the modes of life in different countries, singing, etc., are very interesting to them.

Their conversation is likely to be on frivolous subjects entirely, unless we take the initiative, and by some illustration or happy vein of thought fix their minds upon serious subjects. When this is the case they will listen attentively, and ask questions, and express their own views like sensible creatures. If a desire for learning be awakened, it is surprising how quickly they will learn to read. I have seen gray-haired women bending over the alphabet with patient zeal until they had mastered it. Occasionally we find a woman of marked ability and diligence, and it is a great pleasure to help such in the acquisition of knowledge.

Normal schools have recently been opened in several of the large cities by Government, where women of ability are trained for teaching.

There has been a large increase in girls' schools in India in the last ten years. At the decennial General Missionary Conference, held in Allahabad during Christmas week of 1872, there were statistics given which showed that in 1861 there were fifteen thousand nine hundred and sixty-nine girls' schools in India, and in 1871 there were twenty-six thousand six hundred and seven, showing an increase in ten years of ten thousand six hundred and forty-two.

In the north-west provinces and Oude the ratio has been still greater. There were one thousand three hundred and seven schools in 1861, and in 1871 four thousand two hundred and thirty-two.

Among educated Bengalese, especially the members of the Society called the Brahmo Samaj, there is a strong progressive movement in favor of female education and elevation. Their example, and the encouragement given by Government, are inciting educated natives of all classes to educate their females, and the ratio of increase in schools for them will probably be much greater in 1881.

CHRISTIAN WOMEN.

In Bengal and Southern India, where missions are older than in the north, some women of ability and great devotion have been raised up in the native Churches. To the little province of Coorg, on the Malabar coast, belongs the honor of furnishing the first and, so far, the *only* high-born native lady who has embraced Christianity. The Raja with his daughter, the Princess Gourumna, visited England, and the princess while there made a public profession of her faith in Christ. The Queen of England stood as her sponsor when she was baptized.

In 1873 there was a native Christian lady in Tanjore who died at the age of sixty-two, having spent her life in translating religious books, writing religious poems and hymns, and preaching the Gospel. At her funeral there was a large gathering of people of all classes and creeds, who subsequently agreed to join in erecting a monument to her to express their appreciation of the singular purity and unselfishness of her life.

Native Christian women in the north-west provinces are as yet mostly from the lower ranks of society, and there has been no one of unusual ability among them; but there are many who, according to their ability, are untiring in their efforts to do good to their countrywomen, and many families have been reached and a large amount of teaching carried on by them; and I believe it will be said of many a humble laborer at the last, "She hath done what she could."

Some have "witnessed a good confession" of the sustaining power of Divine grace in the midst of suffering and in the hour of death. A few years ago a sweet-spirited, gentle woman was near her departure from this world, and went to pay a farewell visit at the house of a missionary. She remained to attend evening worship, and when asked to choose a hymn, named one which she said had been in her mind all day. It is called "The Two Homes," and the English version has these beautiful lines:—

"I think upon my earthly home,
And sweet emotions rise;
Yet still my spirit longs to reach
My home above the skies."

The sentiment of the hymn is even more happily brought out in the Hindoostanee version, and she seemed to appropriate it fully. She sang it softly as she was carried home in her palanquin, and the next morning passed gently away to her heavenly home.

I recall to mind, also, a young widow from among the Sikhs who became a Christian and married a catechist. Her life was filled with earnest labors for the good of others, and her departure to the home above was a scene of joyful triumph.

In 1868 there was considerable discussion about teaching the science of medicine to native Christian women in order to fit them for practice among their countrywomen, especially in high-caste families. The subject was brought before some government physicians, and they gave it as their opinion that native women had not sufficient intellect to comprehend the subject.

A native gentleman gave funds to make a trial of the scheme, and a class of twelve Christian women was formed in Nynee Tal. After two years' study and practice they came before some of these same physicians for examination, who expressed surprise and admiration that the class had acquired so much knowledge both of medicine and simple surgery, and gave eight of the women certificates, as follows: "We, the undersigned, have, at the request of the Rev. Dr. Humphrey, examined —— in anatomy, midwifery, pharmacy, practice in medicine, and the management of minor surgical cases, including the more common kinds of fractures and dislocations, and we consider her qualified to practice as a midwife, and also to undertake the treatment of all ordinary diseases. She answered the different questions put to her with remarkable quickness and precision, and in our opinion she has acquired a practical knowledge of medicine and surgery quite equal to the generality of locally-entertained native doctors."

The term "locally entertained" is applied to those doctors who study in government hospitals under the direction of the physicians in charge, and have not attended lectures in a Medical College. The other members of the class, who had not been able to attend so closely to their studies as the others, joined the next class, and two years later also passed a successful examination.

Some of these women are now doing good service as medical Bible readers, finding open doors and a warm welcome wherever they go. Some of them have been taken away in the midst of their usefulness. The most promising one of all, a truly devoted and skillful woman, was stricken down by the sun while prosecuting her humane labors.

Another, after three years of successful labor, has recently gone to her reward. She was not afraid to meet the mysterious change "which *we* call death. She said to her husband as her strength was fast failing, "Let not your heart be troubled, I am going to dwell with my Saviour." When unable to sing herself, she asked her husband to sing the hymn,

"Joyfully, joyfully, onward I move,"

and soon, in quiet assurance of faith, crossed over the river.

A medical class has also been trained in the Girls' Orphanage in Bareilly, under the tuition of Miss Swain, M.D., from which several most useful women have been sent out to various parts of the field.

It is evident, from the foregoing short historical sketches, that the women of India possess powers of mind equal to those of women of any other land ; and since they were capable of so much that was brave and noble, in spite of the depressing influence of Hindooism and Mahomedanism, we may surely expect great things of them when elevated to their true position by Christianity.

The work of making the women of heathendom acquainted with our holy religion belongs most fitly to the women of Christendom, and it is a matter for congratulation that American women are awaking to their high privilege in this respect.

It surely *is* a great and precious privilege to have a part in bringing about the world's redemption, and it ought not to be necessary that harrowing tales of physical suffering and hardship be told in order to incline our hearts to this work. It should be a sufficient call upon our sympathies that the women of heathen lands are ignorant of Christ and of the blessings brought to us through him ; and consequently in the midst of the sorrows and sufferings of earth, they are not cheered and sustained by that hope which is as an anchor to the weary, storm-tossed soul.

There is always ample scope for Christian effort at home, but our sympathies, labors, gifts, and prayers ought not to be confined to our own land, which is already flooded by Gospel light, under whose cheering influence all who desire may come.

There are *armies* of earnest workers here who are striving to advance the cause of truth and righteousness, and are searching in the great mine of humanity for gems to shine in the courts of heaven ; but in heathen lands "the laborers are few," and gems in the rough lie scattered over the mountains and plains, which if gathered and polished would shine with heavenly purity and undying luster.

Let us, then, extend our sympathy to all the dark places of the earth, that we may have some humble part in gathering from heathendom *precious souls*, whose value is immeasurably greater than that of all the treasures of earth, into that glorious kingdom prepared for all true believers in Christ "from the foundation of the world." "And they shall be mine saith the Lord of hosts, in that day when I make up my jewels."